# Physical Characteristic
## Field Spaniel
(from The Kennel Club breed

G000079256

**Colour:** Black, liver or roan. Any one of these with tan markings. Clear black/white or liver/white unacceptable.

**Coat:** Long, flat, glossy and silky in texture. Never curly, short or wiry. Dense and weatherproof. Abundant feathering on chest, under body and behind legs, but clean from hock to ground.

**Tail:** Set on low and never carried above the level of the back. Nicely feathered, with lively action. Customarily docked by one third.

**Hindquarters:** Strong, muscular; stifles moderately bent. Hocks well let down.

**Size:** Height: approximately 45.7 cms (18 ins) at the shoulders. Weight: between 18–25 kgs (40–55 lbs).

# Field Spaniel

◇

*By Becki Jo Hirschy Wolkenheim*

# CONTENTS

All rights reserved.
No part of this book may be reproduced in any form, by photostat, scanner, microfilm, xerography or any other means, or incorporated into any information retrieval system, electronic or mechanical, without the written permission of the copyright owner.
Copyright © 2001 Animalia Books, S.L.
Cover patent pending. Printed in Korea.

PUBLISHED IN THE UNITED KINGDOM BY:

**INTERPET**
PUBLISHING
Vincent Lane, Dorking, Surrey RH4 3YX England

ISBN 1-903098-80-7

PHOTOS BY CAROL ANN JOHNSON

with additional photos by Norvia Behling, Booth Photography, TJ Calhoun, Carolina Biological Supply, David Dalton, Doskocil, Isabelle Français, James Hayden-Yoav, James R Hayden, RBP, Bill Jonas, Dwight R Kuhn, Dr Dennis Kunkel, Mikki Pet Products, Phototake, Jean Claude Revy, Steve Sherouse, Dr Andrew Spielman, Jane Swanson, Tien Tran Photography, Lisa Winters, F E Wolkenheim and L Zobel.

*The publisher wishes to thank the following owners for allowing their dogs to be photographed for this book:* Corkie Goodell, Mrs Hales, Val and Russel Mosedale and Becky Jo Hirschy Wolkenheim

**ACKNOWLEDGEMENT**

Over the past 'almost' two decades, a number of people have freely shared their in-depth knowledge of the Field Spaniel breed with me in candid conversation and wonderful letters: Mrs Peggy Grayson (Westacres), Mrs Margaret Nicholls (Lydemoor-Jonix) and Mrs Win McCann (Pickwick), to whom I am forever grateful for my first Field, 'Clara,' who was allowed to come to my home in 1984. Special thanks also to Mom 'Berd,' sisters Jeni & Wyn, kids Jesse & Mary, Kylie & Steve; friends Janis, Karen & Tom, Jeff & Lanna, Sallys M & H, Eric, Ed & Peggy, Arlene, Kay, Eileen, Liz, Kristy and so many more. I am forever indebted for your support.

The Field Spaniel, as we know it today, originated about 1860, and has been promoted by a small but dedicated fancy.

# History of the
# FIELD SPANIEL

Although the term 'Spanyell' was mentioned in literature as early as 1386, the spaniels involved in the development of the Field Spaniel date to the latter part of the 19th century. The earliest developers envisioned the Field Spaniel as a solid-black spaniel of good size and capable of active hunting.

This was at odds with the preference for spaniels with patches of white in the coat. For working purposes, spaniels with patches of white were considered easier to identify when working in the field. It would be fair to ask, 'If there were already plenty of spaniels to work for hunters, why was there a need for a new spaniel breed?'

One commonly held theory is that the emergence of the dog show in the 1850s may have been a reason behind the initial effort to develop the Field Spaniel in the 1860s as a separate and distinct spaniel breed. Indeed, applying a written standard to describe a perfect physical specimen may well have been a

## DID YOU KNOW?

A spaniel by the name of 'Rover' was traced by Mrs Peggy Grayson in her exhaustive work on the Field Spaniel breed, entitled *The History and Management of the Field Spaniel*, as being shown as both an English Water Spaniel and a Field Spaniel. This dog does not, however, contribute to modern Field Spaniel pedigrees.

**DID YOU KNOW?**
Until 1931, offspring of two varieties
of spaniels mated together could be
registered and subsequently shown as
either variety. After 1931, the
interbred spaniel registry came into
existence. Thereafter, offspring of the
matings of two varieties of spaniels
had to be registered as interbred.

*A 1930 favourite was Mr Owen's Woodbell Perfection, a much-admired Field Spaniel in its day.*

compelling reason to sort out the spaniels one from another.

History shows that the more-or-less formal version of the dog show came into being at about the same time as the emergence of the Field Spaniel as a breed. A large, solid-black spaniel may well have been regarded as a way to win the approval of judges. Thus, the Field Spaniel has often been referred to as a 'manufactured breed.' A remarkable number of varieties of spaniel, some now extinct as distinct breeds, were involved in the evolution of the Field Spaniel.

The modern Field Spaniel owes his foundations to dogs of unremarkable lineage with often-unremarkable names. Spaniels were often classified as either 'land' or 'water' spaniels. Those spaniels classified as land spaniels were equally as often called field spaniels. Though many distinct varieties of land spaniel are recorded in historical documents, these varieties were

*Ch Wribbenhall Waiter was a famous champion during the first decade of the 20th century. This lovely dog was owned by Mr G Mortimer Smith.*

often interbred. Such is the case in the early development of many breeds known today: one variety mated to another variety to produce yet a third variety. For many years, it was not unusual to see littermates registered as the breed they most closely resembled.

Field Spaniels in the early 1900s were very different in appearance from the Field Spaniel seen today. Following its initial development, the Field Spaniel as a breed met with near-disastrous development. It evolved into a dog so long and so low as to be virtually useless in performing the tasks of a gundog. While the dog

show may have contributed to the initial conceptualisation and development of the breed, the dog show is theorised to have also contributed to the decline of the Field Spaniel.

It must be firmly stated that dog shows were a relatively new phenomenon and a hobby for the leisure class. The term 'show dog' was very different in that era in contrast to the modern use of the term. Breeding dogs to show but not to hunt was truly unthinkable.

Dog show judges then, as now, were often unduly influenced by current fads, even fads that called for breed construction that resembled a Basset or Dachshund: excessive body length and short legs. The show rings were full of Field Spaniels with poor structure and, as often tends to happen, type favoured in the show ring tends to drift toward what is currently popular and winning rather than what might be correct.

Reports exist that seem somewhat ludicrous from today's vantage point, which describe judges literally comparing Field Spaniels side-by-side in an apparent effort to determine which exhibit was the longest in body and lowest on leg. This aberrant development of type removed the Field Spaniel far from the original visions of the early developers. The term 'caterpillar dogs' was scathingly used in reference to the breed. The general public who wanted a hunting dog was not impressed and turned away; the Field Spaniel lost his original popularity and has never again regained it.

The extreme version of the breed, which contributed heavily to the near extinction of the Field Spaniel as a distinct spaniel variety, had an appearance that included an excessively long body

**Related to Ch Wribbenhall Waiter is Ch Wribbenhall Whitewash, an outstanding bitch of yesteryear. Initially solid blacks were the rage, then red-and-white or black-and-white with flecking came into favour.**

## GENUS *CANIS*

Dogs and wolves are members of the genus *Canis*. Wolves are known scientifically as *Canis lupus* while dogs are known as *Canis domesticus*. Dogs and wolves are known to interbreed. The term *canine* derives from the Latin derived word *Canis*. The term *dog* has no scientific basis but has been used for thousands of years. The origin of the word 'dog' has never been authoritatively ascertained.

While it is possible to a large extent to 'prove' many breed development theories, interesting evidence exists for the introduction of the Basset Hound in approximately 1880. Written about by prominent dog writers of the day as a foregone conclusion, one can only surmise that perhaps some of those authors had inside information. Although there is no proof that has ever been forthcoming of the cross, it has been generally accepted as fact. This outcross added an array of coat colours never previously seen in such quantity in terms of coloured Fields produced. Predictably, it also resulted in a dog that was shorter on leg while longer in body, and introduced what is popularly called by today's fanciers 'the Basset front' to describe a rather cabriole-

*In the 1880s a Mr W R Bryden, of Beverley in the UK, was a famed breeder of Field Spaniels. Breeders bred longer and lower dogs to meet the demand set by this trend, though such exaggerations eventually undermined the breed's popularity.*

with crooked, short legs, a beautiful yet heavy head and excessive feather. These physical traits were the result of outcrosses, most notably to the long and low Sussex Spaniel. Indeed, some early Field Spaniels had more Sussex Spaniel blood than Field, with some individuals owing three-quarters of their bloodline to Sussex and half-Sussex parents.

*Compare these two heads from dogs of the 1930s. These types, though still appreciated, disappeared from favour as did their solid black colour.*

legged appearance not altogether unknown in modern Fields.

It is perhaps unfair to credit all the long and low Field Spaniels of that era solely to outcrosses to the Sussex Spaniel. While there is one theory that suggests that show ring wins by the longer and lower type of Field Spaniel contributed to the further development of the long and low type of dog, another theory also exists. At the time, sportsmen believed that a spaniel with shorter legs would work thick

into a decline as a direct result of its extreme appearance. The bright side is that the modern Field Spaniel is possessed of an excellent olfactory system and excels in performance events requiring an acute sense of smell. As hounds are renowned for their highly developed scenting abilities, this is pehaps a lucky bit

Woodbell Brigand exemplifies the beautiful dogs so desirable in the 1930s. The Field Spaniel coat may be slightly waved but it must never be curly.

Barum King was supreme in the 1880s, an excellent example of the exaggerations of the period.

cover more effectively than one with relatively longer legs. It was thought that the shorter-legged dog would be slower of pace, work closer to the hunter and would thus be easier for the foot hunter to follow.

Regardless of the reasons for the development of exaggerated type, whether by virtue of breeding longer and lower dogs in order to win in the conformation ring or to produce a different type of hunting spaniel, the breed went

Perhaps the most popular Field Spaniels at the time were produced by Mr G Mortimer Smith, whose Ch Wribbenhall Waterhen is illustrated here.

The Irish Water Spaniel, shown here, is documented as an outcross is certain lines of Field Spaniels, probably contributing its head type to the breed.

of heritage resulting from the Basset Hound outcross.

Evidence of a further outcross to the Irish Water Spaniel has also been documented. Mrs Peggy Grayson makes a startling case for this outcross in her tome on the breed, citing personal letters from a breeder and fancier of the day who claimed that one of his primary bitches contained Irish Water Spaniel blood. It is hard to dispute that this breeder would have stated that his line contained Irish Water Spaniel genes if it did not. Not content to rely solely on this type of written statement, Mrs Grayson examined pedigrees and substantially enhanced the argument that this cross was fact, further theorising that the beautiful and distinctive head of the Field may well be owed to this very outcross. It is plausible to imagine that this took place when one considers the not infrequent predilection of Fields to grow curly topknots, an hallmark of the Irish Water Spaniel.

Madame d'Albany was selected to represent the Field Spaniel characteristics in the 1880s.

Historically, it is undeniably clear and substantiated that the Field Spaniel and the Cocker Spaniel developed together for many years, up until 1901. The two breeds prior to that time were divided almost solely by weight such that solid-coloured animals larger than 25 pounds were recorded as Field Spaniels while those smaller than 25 pounds were recorded as Cocker Spaniels. Hunters certainly cared little that the larger dogs were Fields while their smaller littermates were

In this photo published in 1902, Mr R J Lloyd Price is posing with his Field Spaniel.

The Sussex Spaniel, shown here, was used by Field Spaniel breeders to achieve the lower station and longer legs so desirable in the late 19th century.

Many Field Spaniels are excellent water retrievers and respond with enthusiasm to training for hunting over water.

Cockers. Throughout the earliest development of the breed, varieties of Cocker were utilised in developing the Field, with many of the early fanciers keeping both Cockers and Fields. The liver roan and tan dog, 'Alonzo,' is a dominant dog in early pedigrees for both the modern Field Spaniel and Cocker Spaniel.

Luckily, the Field Spaniel was rescued from its initial slide toward extinction by fanciers who had the good sense to reflect upon the original type envisioned by the developers of the breed. While knowledgeable dog writers were claiming the breed to be certain to dwindle toward extinction, the next outcrosses were to bring in English Springer Spaniel genes to restore a more upstanding type of dog. Sportsmen of the day, who desired a strong spaniel to work thick and formidable cover, persisted in crossing Fields with English Springer Spaniels, with attention focused mostly on the working ability of the offspring. The last such outcross was recorded in the mid-1950s. This, of course, introduced obvious coloration traits such that the breed standard at one point was deliberately changed to preclude black and white or liver and white exhibits from winning, colours definitely associated with the Springer. This was in an effort to distinguish between the English Springer Spaniel and the Field Spaniel. The breed was larger and longer in leg while still retaining the substance, movement and characteristic head of the Field Spaniel. Perhaps this was, after all, as the original developers of the 1860s had envisioned.

Despite a small revival, as World War II approached, the breed was once again in trouble. Managing to maintain just a toehold on survival, the Field Spaniel progressed precariously during the 1940s. Remaining so few in number that the survival of the Field Spaniel as a distinct breed is somewhat miraculous, registrations climbed sporadically. This pattern continued throughout much of the

**BRAIN AND BRAWN**

Since dogs have been inbred for centuries, their physical and mental characteristics are constantly being changed to suit man's desires for hunting, retrieving, scenting, guarding and warming their masters' laps. During the past 150 years, dogs have been judged according to physical characteristics as well as functional abilities. Few breeds can boast a genuine balance between physique, working ability and temperament.

1950s and into the mid-1960s. The Field Spaniel simply would not be extinguished and began to slowly rise from the ashes yet again.

All modern Field Spaniels descend directly from two dogs and two bitches through two important litters of the late 1960s. These Field Spaniels were Ronayne Regal and Gormac Teal, littermates of the black coat colour, whelped in 1962; Columbina of Teffont, a black bitch, whelped in 1957; and Elmbury Morwenna of Rhiwlas, a liver-coloured bitch, whelped in 1963. In extending the pedigree of any modern Field Spaniel, these four dogs will be found: a remarkably narrow genetic base.

Ronayne Regal figures prominently in modern Field pedigrees through his son, the liver-coloured Ridware Emperor, and daughter, the black-coloured Sh Ch Mittina Ridware Samantha, both out of Columbina of Teffont. Regal's littermate, Gormac Teal, figures prominently as he sired perhaps the two most famous litters of the modern history of the Field Spaniel. These were the 'J' litter from Mittina in 1968, out of Sh Ch Mittina Ridware Samantha, and the 'A' litter that was produced under the Elmbury affix in 1969 out of Juno of Elmbury (Ridware Emperor x Elmbury Morwenna of Rhiwlas). You will find 'J' and 'A' ancestors behind all present-day Field Spaniels. It is at once obvious how very narrow is the genetic base of the modern Field Spaniel. While fanciers in other breeds may speak of a gene pool, Field Spaniels truly began from a gene puddle! This fact must be kept in mind by anyone who would endeavour to breed future generations of Field Spaniels.

Today's Field Spaniels are not as exaggerated as were dogs in the breed's past. Dogs with overdone physical characteristics do poorly in the field.

The Field Spaniel is highly intelligent and loyal, excelling as a home companion, hunting dog and competition dog.

# *Characteristics of the*

# FIELD SPANIEL

'Fields are fun!' is a saying reproduced on numerous T-shirts worn by breed aficionados in the United States. Worldwide, this statement seems to draw unanimous agreement. Stories of Field Spaniels' exploits are legend among those who are fortunate enough to live with them. Their highly developed sense of humour is renowned, and Field Spaniels seem to love having the last laugh. Typically good-natured, loyal to family and highly intelligent, the Field Spaniel thrives when included in virtually all everyday activities; indeed, he expects that his family will include him!

The breed is also renowned for a natural reserve in temperament. Somewhat aloof in initial meetings with strangers, Field Spaniels are at the same time not indifferent. It is as if they simply prefer to look the situation over and reach their own conclusion as to whether or not an individual is worthy of friendship. That Field Spaniels have a perceptive sense in assessing

If one Field Spaniel is fun, imagine the pleasure of owning, training and showing five dogs at the same time....not to mention the time and commitment!

people is a belief strongly affirmed by those who own them. A reserved reaction in initial introductions is strikingly different from a shy temperament that should never be tolerated in the breed.

Both males and females exhibit similar personality traits. Many fanciers, however, do remark on a predisposition of the males to be a bit more willing to snuggle. Females, while also sweet, may be a bit more independent in nature. Field Spaniels get along well with children and other household animals provided they are positively exposed to these while young. The memory of the breed is long, and negative associations may be difficult to overcome without concerted effort. Thus, interactions of a puppy with young children must be supervised. Common sense must prevail when introducing an impressionable puppy to your household.

'Determined' is another word often used in describing the Field Spaniel. Perhaps this very tenacity is what helped the breed survive its rather precarious climb from near extinction; it most certainly renders the breed a very suitable companion for hunting and many other performance pursuits. This is a different

**Visiting Fields at a kennel is an exciting and enlightening way to get to know this remarkable breed.**

### DO YOU WANT TO LIVE LONGER?

If you like to volunteer, it is wonderful if you can take your dog to a nursing home once a week for several hours. The elder community loves to have a dog with which to visit, and often your dog will bring a bit of companionship to someone who is lonely or somewhat detached from the world. You will be not only bringing happiness to someone else but also keeping your dog busy—and we haven't even mentioned the fact that it has been discovered that volunteering helps to increase your own longevity!

trait from stubbornness or hard-headedness; rather, think in terms of steadfastness and persistence in reaching a goal such as flushing a bird that is difficult to rout from thick cover.

Training does not require heavy-handed tactics. The breed is relatively easy to train with positive motivation for the most part in the form of praise, food treats and games played with their owners. Field Spaniels will thoroughly enjoy such rewards. For example, when you are happy to leave a good game of retrieve in the garden, your Field Spaniel may not be content to do so. The result may be the dog's then wandering from person to person with a tennis ball or stick

in search of continuing the game. A new Field Spaniel owner described a rather hilarious situation in which a ready-to-play puppy persisted in presenting the family cat with a tennis ball. The cat, of course, was not amused, staring at the ceiling, as cats are wont to do when ignoring something or someone! This natural penchant for play may be exploited in training the dog; keep training enjoyable and the Field Spaniel is likely to respond as if saying, 'Whatever the game, I'll play.'

The drinking and eating behaviour of the breed is the source of much comedy, provided the owner has a healthy sense of humour. Fields drinking water are prone to 'sharing,' such that a partial mouthful of water is often trailed to and from the water dish. Further, dinnertime is an eagerly anticipated daily event for the Field, as it is rare to find one who is a finicky eater. The Field enjoys his dinner with gusto. Using food rewards is a natural way to proceed in training many behaviours when introducing the dog to the family lifestyle. So dedicated are they to eating that Field Spaniels will beg at the dinner table and become food thieves if this behaviour is tolerated. Stories abound of disappearing dinner roasts and very happily satiated Field Spaniels.

## TAKING CARE

Science is showing that as people take care of their pets, the pets are taking care of their owners. A study in 1998, published in the *American Journal of Cardiology,* found that having a pet can prolong his owner's life. Pet owners generally have lower blood pressure, and pets help their owners to relax and keep more physically fit. It was also found that pets help to keep the elderly connected to their communities.

**HEART HEALTHY**

The *Australian Medical Journal* in 1992 found that having pets is heart-healthy. Pet owners had lower blood pressure and lower levels of triglycerides than those who didn't have pets. It has also been found that senior citizens who own pets are more active and less likely to experience depression than those without pets.

Such 'thievery' may be extended to any items routinely handled or favoured by owners. This is not typically, as it might seem on the surface, a case of simple destructiveness. On the contrary, it is generally a Field Spaniel's tribute to how highly the dog values his human pack. Items frequently used by humans pick up the smell of a well-loved human, becoming a prize in the mind of the Field Spaniel. Library books, remote-control devices and clothing that has been worn and not yet washed are items that the Field Spaniel will find intriguing to pick up, play with and carry.

The breed does shed and this results in fluff-balls of hair that settle overnight. Moderate shedding occurs year-round while heavier shedding is predictable during warmer months. Regular brushing is required to remove dead hair and reduce the amount of sweeping necessary in one's household. Furthermore, the Field Spaniel is not adverse to mud and other outdoor elements that will enthusiastically be tracked back into the household. The Field Spaniel is not a breed for a person with 'house beautiful' aspirations. However, the breed's natural desire for training and pleasing its owner means that a Field Spaniel can be gently and kindly taught proper home manners. Your Field will learn to wait at the door to have his paws wiped and to expect the owner to wipe his face after eating (before he wipes it on the sofa). Both routines and similar ones are relatively easy to establish.

The vocal range of the breed is the stuff of legend. Field Spaniels are capable of and readily use a wide variety of vocal expressions, ranging from a deep-throated bark to high-pitched squeals, distinctive yodels, yips and howls. This is how the Field communicates his pleasure or displeasure, often interacting with his owners in a manner that is nearly human in his ability to express his emotions. In addition, many Field Spaniels snore during slumber. This can, of course, be mildly annoying when the Field sleeps in your bedroom.

The very intelligence of the breed can and does contribute to behaviours that develop quickly and can be difficult to extinguish, particularly if the dog has been gratified in some way for the behaviour. For example, a puppy who is allowed to jump up on his owners in greeting will not realise that the owner is one day dressed in fine clothes and will not make the connection that jumping up might present a problem. Since all previous greetings of this sort received pats, hugs and happy vocal praise from their owner, it is only to be expected that the Field Spaniel would remember and seek to perpetuate the usual routine.

Field Spaniel exploits in discovering how to work their environment to their advantage are legend. Fields investigating the home bathroom have been known to discover how to lift the lid of a toilet for a drink of water or even turn on faucets! One Field Spaniel inadvertently lifted the latch of a door and discovered his own ability to go in and out of the house. In this particular case, even after the latch was changed to a doorknob, the Field would routinely check—every so often—just to see if, by chance, he would be able to open that door once again. Field Spaniel owners must indeed have a sense of humour and see things as the dog sees them, since, after all, the good-natured Field Spaniel truly thinks life is to be enjoyed to the fullest.

## DOGS, DOGS, GOOD FOR YOUR HEART!

People usually purchase dogs for companionship, but studies show that dogs can help to improve their owners' health and level of activity, as well as lower a human's risk of coronary heart disease. Without even realising it, when a person puts time into exercising, grooming and feeding a dog, he also puts more time into his own personal health care. Dog owners establish more routine schedules for their dogs to follow, which can have positive effects on a human's health. Dogs also teach us patience, offer unconditional love and provide the joy of having a furry friend to pet!

# Breed Standard for the

# FIELD SPANIEL

## INTRODUCTION TO THE BREED STANDARD

Fanciers share the common goal to produce a Field Spaniel of correct type, beautiful enough to win in the show ring, yet imbued with innate ability and trainability to work in the field. Indeed, the ideal Field Spaniel is a versatile companion, well suited to many activities. It is important to remember the precarious and colourful history of the Field Spaniel breed. All the different varieties that created the breed in the beginning, and the necessity for outcrosses to the English Springer Spaniel to avoid extinction, will account for variation in type seen today as these genes line up. It is not unknown, for example, to see Field Spaniels who have a hint, and sometimes more, of Sussex or English Springer Spaniel appearance to the head and body. On occasion, a 'houndy' head will arise and, more often, a shorter hound-type coat will appear. Knowledge of the breed standard is mandatory for those who would endeavour to breed and show the Field Spaniel.

While the name 'Field Spaniel' is one that somewhat lacks in distinction and often causes confusion, the breed is anything but nondescript. The term 'moderate' is one used in the standard of the breed and sometimes causes confusion, as the perception of what is moderate and what is not has a great deal of variation. When looking at the Field Spaniel, one is immediately drawn to the beauty of the head. Even so, the Field Spaniel should not be described as a 'head breed,' whose virtues are solely resting on the construction of the head, since the overall proportion, balance, depth and bone of the body contribute equally as much to the distinctive appearance of the breed. To emphasise one attribute at the expense of another does the breed no service.

There are a number of official breed standards for the Field Spaniel, including the one recognised by The Kennel Club of Great Britain and the

American Kennel Club standard, as well as Canadian and Australian standards. Most standards, including the Fédération Cynologique Internationale (FCI) standard, reflect The Kennel Club standard. The author here paints a portrait of the breed that reflects the content of all these standards, a true international rendering of this beautiful breed.

## A PORTRAIT OF THE IDEAL FIELD SPANIEL

In considering the proper Field Spaniel head, one is first drawn to the overall impression of nobility and character that are part and parcel of the breed. The Field Spaniel head is very different from that of other spaniel breeds and there should never be a doubt in the eye of the beholder that one is looking at a Field Spaniel. Even those not well acquainted with the breed will say things such as 'I knew this wasn't an "xyz" spaniel,' where 'xyz' stands for the name of a breed with which they were familiar.

The head of the Field Spaniel is at once striking. Framed by low-set, long ears with a good amount of silky feathering, the face is animated by brown eyes of various shades that suit the coat colour and that are at once lively, yet gentle. The brows should be distinctly apparent

The present-day Field Spaniel is the picture of moderation, showing no signs of exaggeration. The British proudly extend this rule to the grooming of the breed as well.

An American-bred Field Spaniel in magnificent condition, showing off his more refined (and clippered) appearance.

and expressive above somewhat widely spaced eyes that are neither loose nor round and protruding. The skull should give the overall impression of length and rectangular appearance when viewed from the side or the top, beginning at the occiput to the tip of the nose. The length of muzzle is never shorter than the length of the backskull and the nasal bone is straight. The lips must fit the muzzle well, without any hint of being pendulous, so that the view of the muzzle from the side is one of soft and gradual curves.

Beneath and above the eyes, the face is aristocratically chiselled, with cheekbones that are relatively flat. The brow is not heavy or has no tendency to overshadow the eyes, blending gradually between the eyes into the foreface. The stop, as the area is called between the mid-brow and the muzzle, should be apparent but never steep. The nose colour must be solid and tone with the coat colour of the dog—brown for liver animals (darker is generally considered preferable by fanciers) and black for Fields of the black coat colour. In addition, the nose should be very large with wide-open nostrils and set onto the end of the muzzle without any upward or downward turning; this is, after all, a breed that uses its nose in finding game, and the

**MALE VS. FEMALE**
Mature males will typically be larger than females in both height and weight, although still within the stated standard for the breed. In other words, if the stated uppermost range is 55 pounds, then the males are more likely to be closer to the upper end of the range and the females more likely to be nearer the lower end of the range. The difference is similar for height; males tend to be taller than females.

large nose and straight nasal bone enhance scenting ability.

The entire head sets onto a neck of good length. A slight arch to the neck from behind the occiput adds to the aristocratic, finely bred appearance when the animal is viewed from the side.

**THE IDEAL SPECIMEN**
According to The Kennel Club, 'The
Breed Standard is the "Blueprint" of
the ideal specimen in each breed
approved by a governing body, e.g.
The Kennel Club, the Fédération
Cynologique Internationale (FCI) and
the American Kennel Club.

'The Kennel Club writes and revises
Breed Standards taking account of the
advice of Breed Councils/Clubs.
Breed Standards are not changed
lightly to avoid "changing the
standard to fit the current dogs" and
the health and well-being of future
dogs is always taken into account
when new standards are prepared or
existing ones altered.'

The length of the neck should be sufficient so that, when trailing game, the dog does not appear to droop at the shoulder, and that objects to be retrieved are easily picked up off the ground. From the front, the skin of the neck should be well fitted, with just enough suppleness that it is able to roll, rather than tear, when the animal is working the dense cover for which he was bred.

The front legs are set well beneath the body of the Field Spaniel, and the prosternum (the foremost portion of the chest structure) is readily apparent and there is no hint of flatness. The length of the shoulder blade and upper arm should be nearly identical; short upper arms create undesirable short-strided front movement, which is easily outpowered by strong drive of the rear legs, thereby creating a side-winding-type movement. The stride must begin in the shoulder as the legs are driven forward, and imbalance between the length of the shoulder bone and the upper arm will create an inefficient gait. There must be good space between the front legs, never less than a hand-span on an adult dog, yet, at the same time, not so wide as to give any hint of protruding elbows when viewed from the front. Ideal front movement when viewed from the side shows excellent forward reach of the front legs with no hint of choppiness or high-stepping hackneyed movement.

The overall impression of the Field Spaniel body when viewed from the side should at once be that of a good size, though not massive spaniel, with just a hint (and no more) of length, and a good depth to the body that begins at the chest and continues through the loin. From top of the back to the chest should be approximate to the distance from bottom of the chest to the ground. Overly deep chests, such that the dog appears to have rather less length of leg, or those which are shallow, such that the dog appears to have great length of leg, are not correct. Balance here is the key. The impression of bone should be that it is neither too little nor too much for the overall body. This is a large spaniel in terms of overall body substance without excessive height, and the legs must have sufficient size to support the body. While legs that appear too spindly to support the body are not desirable, neither are legs so thick as to resemble miniature tree trunks, as this massiveness will inhibit working speed.

The topline must be level and firm during movement or when standing still. Both dips in the centre of the back, such that the appearance is reminiscent of an old work horse, and roaching, such that the back appears like that of a racing hound, must be avoided at all costs, as these will lead to a dog who tires more easily during activity. The framework of bone that lies beneath and supports the topline is important to assess. It is the overall length of rib that contributes to the very slightly longer profile of the breed. When drawing an imaginary line from prosternum to the end of the rib cage that is horizontal to the ground, the ideal length of this line accounts for nearly two-thirds of the overall body length. Fields with short rib cages will often have an immediately noticeable sharp upward curve of

loin, or 'tuck-up,' that rises to create a distinct waist. In these cases, the width of the loin is almost always too long or else the overall dog is more square than slightly rectangular. In addition, shorter rib cages tend to go 'barrelled'—an appearance

### BREEDING CONSIDERATIONS
The decision to breed your dog is one that must be considered carefully and researched thoroughly before moving into action. Some people believe that breeding will make their bitches happier or that it is an easy way to make money. Unfortunately, indiscriminate breeding only worsens the rampant problem of pet overpopulation, as well as putting a considerable dent in your pocketbook. As for the bitch, the entire process from mating through whelping is not an easy one and puts your pet under considerable stress. Last, but not least, consider whether or not you have the means to care for an entire litter of pups. Without a reputation in the field, your attempts to sell the pups may be unsuccessful.

Responsible breeders strive to produce healthy, temperamentally sound puppies that will grow up to embody the breed standard as closely as possible.

that is more round than ideal and easily seen when viewing the animal from the top. The loin must be only gently perceptible, though this often comes with age, and puppies up to two and even three years of age may have a more noticeable break in the loin.

The area in which the tail is set onto the body is ideally a natural extension of the line of the back, without any sloping to the croup, as the tail is, after all, an extension of the bony framework of the spine itself. There is no concave dimple where the tail leaves the body as this indicates a tail that is set on too low. At the same time, the tail should not be set overly high so that it is carried well above the line of the back. The tail of the Field Spaniel is customarily docked within a few days of birth, though the standards of some countries allow for natural tails and there are a number of countries that prohibit any docking. Though it is safe to say that the vast majority of Field Spaniel breeders do dock tails,

dogs with undocked tails have been successfully shown to championship titles. When docked, care must be taken to avoid a dock that is overly short. In general, one-third of the overall tail length is retained. In the case of tails, it is better to err on the side of leaving too much rather than too little.

The rear legs should immediately convey the impression of great strength and a well-developed, muscular thigh. Angles of the upper and lower leg are moderate such that the entire assembly of the rear leg does not require great backward extension to level the topline as, for example, when the dog is posed for the show ring. Beneath the hock joint, the rear pasterns are short and provide for a powerful characteristic stride that at once appears effortless while propelling the dog forward. In no case should

### BREEDER'S BLUEPRINT

If you are considering breeding your bitch, it is very important that you are familiar with the breed standard. Reputable breeders breed with the intention of producing dogs that are as close as possible to the standard and that contribute to the advancement of the breed. Study the standard for both physical appearance and temperament, and make certain your bitch and your chosen stud dog measure up.

the rear leg movement interfere with that of the front legs as this will lead to flaws in movement, i.e. inefficiency for covering ground without fatigue. When viewing the dog moving in a trotting gait from the side, one should be thoroughly convinced that the dog could maintain the pace all day.

The feet of the Field Spaniel are what endear him to many fanciers. While puppies of many breeds appear to have feet that are large and need to be 'grown into,' the Field Spaniel carries this appearance for a lifetime. Large feet, with thick pads and well-arched toes that do not spread apart or become flattened in appearance when the dog stands or moves, are ideally made for the most daunting cover when working—or playing—outdoors. These large webbed feet are also ideal for propelling the Field Spaniel through water. Though most Fields are born with dewclaws on the front legs, a few are known to have dewclaws on the rear legs as well. Dewclaws are generally removed within a few days of birth, as they are prone to snagging later in life, which may result in painful injury.

The Field Spaniel is clothed in a thick and weatherproof coat of silky texture. There is feathering on the ears, backs of the front and rear legs, and beneath the belly, but never so much as to even approach the ground in length. Dogs in the

The Field Spaniel has a coat that is thick and weatherproof with a silky texture.

show rings typically have longer feathering than those that work the field.

The coat comes in a variety of colours, though this is not without controversy! Considered a solid-coloured dog in that the base coat colour covers the entire dog, the most commonly seen colours are liver and black. The liver coat is seen in a variety of shades from that of a milk chocolate to a dark chocolate colour. Hints of gold in a light liver colour coat are thought by many to be a throwback to the great amount of Sussex Spaniel blood introduced to the breed during its early development. Patches of white may appear on the chests of liver or black Field Spaniels, though nowhere else without penalty in the show ring. In this case, less is typically viewed more favourably and any white that extends from shoulder to shoulder in width (a 'shirtfront') is definitely too much. Many fanciers actually prefer just a stripe or line of white dusting down the chest. Tan points may be seen on any coat colour (including roan), appearing on the eyebrows, sides of the muzzle (sometimes extending back to the cheeks), chest, front and rear pasterns and a typical patch beneath the tail. Ideally, the tan is a rich golden colour and not washed out in appear-ance, and there may be dark 'pencil' marks on the toes that only serve to enhance the tan colouring.

The roan coloration is perhaps where the most contro-versy exists in terms of how the term 'roan' is defined. There is much disagreement among fanciers as to the proper defini-tion of the term. While some fanciers define 'roan' as an intermingling of coloured and white hairs such that the dog may take on a 'silvered' appear-ance while having some patches of dark coat colour, most commonly on the head and back, other fanciers expand the defini-tion. Dogs with tiny ticking spots in a base white coat colour, to the point that dogs may appear to be black and white or liver and white until one ruffles the coat to determine that there is intermingling of the coloured and white hairs, are also defined as 'roan' by some breeders. There is, at this point, a fairly even split among those using either definition so that the somewhat muddy definition of the term 'roan' is likely to be present for some time to come. Coat colour is the least important attribute among the abilities of a Field Spaniel as a companion in one's home or a hunter extraordinaire, though it sometimes has a bearing on how well a dog does in the show ring.

## SELECTING A FIELD PUPPY

In choosing a Field Spaniel puppy, first and foremost consider your aspirations in acquiring a Field Spaniel. Do you wish to show your dog in the conformation ring? Do you want a superb bird dog? Do you want a household companion? Or, do you—as do many who choose the Field Spaniel—want a dog that can do all of these? While faults, such as too much white on the chest or a head style that varies too far from standard, may effectively rule a puppy out as a show prospect, faults of this nature are not likely to make a difference for a Field Spaniel whose primary occupation will be as a hunting partner or household companion. Most Field Spaniel litters have an amount of variation within the litter in terms of type, personality and even size; it is rare that all puppies in any single litter would be show prospects or that all puppies would show the interest in birds desirable in a hunting companion. Know what your goals are before you begin contacting breeders; this will be helpful to the breeder in determining if there is an appropriate puppy for you in any particular litter.

Once you know what your goals are in acquiring a puppy, the next important aspect to

### PUPPY SELECTION

Your selection of a good puppy can be determined by your needs. A show potential or a good pet? It is your choice. Every puppy, however, should be of good temperament. Although show-quality puppies are bred and raised with emphasis on physical conformation, responsible breeders strive for equally good temperament. Do not buy from a breeder who concentrates solely on physical beauty at the expense of personality.

**PUPPY APPEARANCE**
Your puppy should have a well-fed appearance but not a distended abdomen, which may indicate worms or incorrect feeding, or both. The body should be firm, with a solid feel. The skin of the abdomen should be pale pink and clean, without signs of scratching or rash. Check the hind legs to make certain that dewclaws were removed, if any were present at birth.

may produce a puppy who will show problems. Fortunately, health problems known in the Field Spaniel breed are fewer in number in comparison with many other breeds, particularly in consideration of the narrow genetic base of the breed. General good health seems to be a trait with which the breed, overall, is fortunate to be endowed. However, there are concerns that appear often enough to warrant discussion with breeders.

*Hip dysplasia:* Hip dysplasia is an abnormal development of the ball and socket apparatus of the hip joint, which is typically progressive with the growth and development of the puppy to the adult dog. Symptoms have wide variation, from almost none

**INSURANCE**
Many good breeders will offer you insurance with your new puppy, which is an excellent idea. The first few weeks of insurance will probably be covered free of charge or with only minimal cost, allowing you to take up the policy when this expires. If you own a pet dog, it is sensible to take out such a policy as veterinary fees can be high, although routine vaccinations and boosters are not covered. Look carefully at the many options open to you before deciding which suits you best.

consider is overall health. After all, you will have this Field Spaniel for the next dozen or more years and nothing can break the heart more quickly than a well-loved puppy that is not sound in body or mind. Much to the dismay of concerned Field Spaniel breeders worldwide, even the most cautious breeding of two parents testing normal for all known 'testable' problems perceptible to extreme pain and lameness. Virtually every country where Field Spaniels reside has veterinary schemes available to rate the conformation of the hip joint. While it is not a fail-safe prevention, as factors other than heredity come into play, research data worldwide concludes that breeding two parents with 'normal' hip conformation tends to produce a higher percentage of puppies with 'normal' hip conformation.

*Eye abnormalities:* These include entropion (eyelids that turn inward), ectropion (eyelids that are turn somewhat outward to create a loose eye showing haw) and cataracts. PRA or progressive retinal atrophy is another condition diagnosed in Field Spaniels that leads to total blindness; luckily, there have been very few dogs reliably diagnosed with this particular disorder. Many eye abnormalities are considered genetically transferred, and breeding two parents with 'normal' eyes tends to produce a higher percentage of puppies with 'normal' eyes.

*Hypothyroidism:* Low levels of thyroid hormones have been well known in the breed for a number of years and are thought by many veterinary researchers to contribute to other auto-immune disorders. While there is some controversy over the heritable nature of the problem, it is safe to

**PREPARING FOR PUP**
Unfortunately, when a puppy is bought by someone who does not take into consideration the time and attention that dog ownership requires, it is the puppy who suffers when he is either abandoned or placed in a shelter by a frustrated owner. So all of the 'homework' you do in preparation for your pup's arrival will benefit you both. The more informed you are, the more you will know what to expect and the better equipped you will be to handle the ups and downs of raising a puppy. Hopefully, everyone in the household is willing to do his part in raising and caring for the pup. The anticipation of owning a dog often brings a lot of promises from excited family members: 'I will walk him every day,' 'I will feed him,' 'I will housebreak him,' etc., but these things take time and effort, and promises can easily be forgotten once the novelty of the new pet has worn off.

If you aspire to show your Field Spaniel in conformation, you must make your wishes clear to the breeder from whom you purchase your pup.

# DO YOU KNOW ABOUT HIP DYSPLASIA?

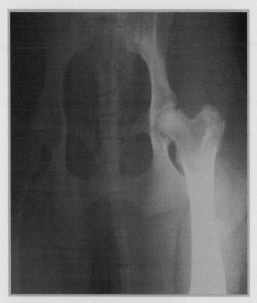

**X-ray of a dog with 'Good' hips.**

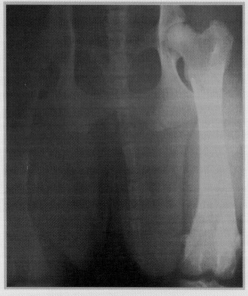

**X-ray of a dog with 'Moderate' dysplastic hips.**

Hip dysplasia is a fairly common condition found in purebred dogs. When a dog has hip dysplasia, its hind leg has an incorrectly formed hip joint. By constant use of the hip joint, it becomes more and more loose, wears abnormally and may become arthritic.

Hip dysplasia can only be confirmed with an x-ray, but certain symptoms may indicate a problem. Your dog may have a hip dysplasia problem if it walks in a peculiar manner, hops instead of smoothly runs, uses his hind legs in unison (to keep the pressure off the weak joint), has trouble getting up from a prone position or always sits with both legs together on one side of its body.

As the dog matures, it may adapt well to life with a bad hip, but in a few years the arthritis develops and many dogs with hip dysplasia become cripples.

Hip dysplasia is considered an inherited disease and only can be diagnosed definitively when the dog is two years old. Some experts claim that a special diet might help your puppy outgrow the bad hip, but the usual treatments are surgical. The removal of the pectineus muscle, the removal of the round part of the femur, reconstructing the pelvis and replacing the hip with an artificial one are all surgical interventions that are expensive, but they are usually very successful. Follow the advice of your veterinary surgeon.

say that breeding two parents with 'normal' thyroid function is likely to produce a higher percentage of puppies who will also have 'normal' thyroid function. That said, hypothyroidism is among the most treatable of any problem, involving annual blood testing and inexpensive daily medication.

It is possible to get a 'feel' for the general health of a breeder's stock by visiting the kennel if at all possible. Realistically, this is not always something that can be done given the rarity of the breed and the various locations of breeders. For example, show prospects may be imported from one country to another, and in some countries such as the United States, obtaining a Field Spaniel puppy may well mean that the puppy must travel by airplane from one coast to the other! In these cases, you will need to do most of your investigation by telephone. Ask questions about the health, temperament and ages of parents, and then go on to ask about grandparents and great-grandparents. Did these dogs live to older ages or did they die young? What health problems has the breeder encountered in previous litters? Be wary of any breeder who has bred more than a litter or two who flatly states they have never produced a dog with any sort of

**DID YOU KNOW?**
You should not even think about buying a puppy that looks sick, undernourished, overly frightened or nervous. Sometimes a timid puppy will warm up to you after a 30-minute 'let's-get-acquainted' session.

problem! If you are fortunate enough to be able to visit the breeder, look at and interact with the dogs residing with the breeder and assess their overall appearance, i.e. are these the type of dogs with whom you wish to live?

Reviewing pedigrees can be helpful in some instances. For example, if your goal is a show dog that you hope will win in the conformation ring, check for depth over several generations of champions in the pedigree. Similarly, if your goal is a hunting companion, look for evidence of proven hunting ability in the pedigree, such as Field Champions or Working Trial awards.

If you are fortunate enough to be able to visit a litter in person, approach the visitation with your head and not your heart. The puppy that is extremely reticent may tug at your heart, but may not be the best prospect if you have a busy household or you wish to have a dog that virtually shouts 'look at me' to a dog show judge. On the other hand, this same puppy with a reticent but gentle nature may be the ideal companion in other situations.

### DID YOU KNOW?

Breeders rarely release puppies until they are eight to ten weeks of age. This is an acceptable age for most breeds of dog, excepting toy breeds, which are not released until around 12 weeks, given their petite sizes. If a breeder has a puppy that is 12 weeks of age or older, it is likely well socialised and housetrained. Be sure that it is otherwise healthy before deciding to take it home.

### DOCUMENTATION

Two important documents you will get from the breeder are the pup's pedigree and registration certificate. The breeder should register the litter and each pup with The Kennel Club, and it is necessary for you to have the paperwork if you plan on showing or breeding in the future.

Make sure you know the breeder's intentions on which type of registration he will obtain for the pup. There are limited registrations which may prohibit the dog from being shown, bred or competing in non-conformation trials such as Working or Agility if the breeder feels that the pup is not of sufficient quality to do so. There is also a type of registration that will permit the dog in non-conformation competition only.

On the reverse side of the registration certificate, the new owner can find the transfer section, which must be signed by the breeder.

Look for obvious signs of health: eyes should be clear without tearing, there should be no obvious structural problems such as lameness, there should be no coughing or raspiness to the breathing, and the overall litter should simply have the appearance of health and good nature—physically clean and accustomed to being handled by people.

Finally, as you are interviewing the breeder, be prepared to have the breeder interview you! Field Spaniel breeders are generally a cautious lot and care deeply about the placement of each individual puppy in the proper home for that puppy. Be prepared for some in-depth questions about your home, your overall experience with dogs and so forth. Give honest answers, as this will assist the breeder greatly in determining if there is a puppy in the litter that will suit your home and goals. A good match of an individual puppy and owner is essential to a happy dog-owner relationship.

**COMMITMENT OF OWNERSHIP**
After considering all of these factors, you have most likely already made some very

**BOY OR GIRL?**
An important consideration to be discussed is the sex of your puppy. For a family companion, a bitch may be the better choice, considering the female's inbred concern for all young creatures and her accompanying tolerance and patience. It is always advisable to spay a pet bitch, which may guarantee her a longer life.

**YOUR SCHEDULE . . .**
If you lead an erratic, unpredictable life, with daily or weekly changes in your work requirements, consider the problems of owning a puppy. The new puppy has to be fed regularly, socialised (loved, petted, handled, introduced to other people) and, most importantly, allowed to visit outdoors for toilet training. As the dog gets older, it can be more tolerant of deviations in its feeding and toilet relief.

important decisions about selecting your puppy. You have chosen a Field Spaniel, which means that you have decided which characteristics you want in a dog and what type of dog will best fit into your family and lifestyle. If you have selected a breeder, you have gone a step further—you have done your research and found a responsible, conscientious person who breeds quality Field Spaniels and who

should be a reliable source of
help as you and your puppy
adjust to life together. If you have
observed a litter in action, you
have obtained a firsthand look at
the dynamics of a puppy 'pack'
and, thus, you should learn about
each pup's individual personality—perhaps you have even
found one that particularly
appeals to you.

However, even if you have
not yet found the Field Spaniel
puppy of your dreams, observing
pups will help you learn to
recognise certain behaviour and
to determine what a pup's
behaviour indicates about his
temperament. You will be able to
pick out which pups are the
leaders, which ones are less
outgoing, which ones are
confident, which ones are shy,
playful, friendly, aggressive, etc.
Equally as important, you will
learn to recognise what a healthy
pup should look and act like. All
of these things will help you in
your search, and when you find
the Field Spaniel that was meant
for you, you will know it!

Researching your breed,
selecting a responsible breeder
and observing as many pups as
possible are all important steps
on the way to dog ownership. It
may seem like a lot of effort...and
you have not even taken the pup
home yet! Remember, though,
you cannot be too careful when it
comes to deciding on the type of

dog you want and finding out about your prospective pup's background. Buying a puppy is not—or should not be—just another whimsical purchase. This is one instance in which you actually do get to choose your own family! You may be thinking that buying a puppy should be fun—it should not be so serious and so much work. Keep in mind that your puppy is not a cuddly stuffed toy or decorative lawn ornament, but a creature that will become a real member of your family. You will come to realise that, while buying a puppy is a pleasurable and exciting endeavour, it is not something to be taken lightly. Relax...the fun will start when the pup comes home!

Always keep in mind that a puppy is nothing more than a baby in a furry disguise...a baby who is virtually helpless in a human world and who trusts his owner for fulfilment of his basic needs for survival. In addition to water and shelter, your pup needs care, protection, guidance and love. If you are not prepared to commit to this, then you are not prepared to own a dog.

It is the author's intention to emphasise the commitment of dog ownership as the Field Spaniel truly requires an active, interactive owner. Certainly, with some time and patience, you will raise a curious and exuberant

**In the hands of dedicated breeders, the Field Spaniel is lovingly maintained and bred for consistency and soundness. With a little effort, you can locate a healthy, well-bred puppy.**

Field Spaniel pup to be a well-adjusted and well-mannered adult dog—a dog that could be your most loyal friend.

## PREPARING PUPPY'S PLACE IN YOUR HOME

Researching your breed and finding a breeder are only two aspects of the 'homework' you will have to do before taking your Field Spaniel puppy home. You will also have to prepare your home and family for the new addition. Much as you would prepare a nursery for a newborn baby, you will need to designate a place in your home that will be the puppy's own. How you prepare your home will depend on how much freedom the dog will be allowed. Whatever you decide, you must ensure that he has a place that he can 'call his own.'

When you bring your new puppy into your home, you are bringing him into what will become his home as well. Obviously, you did not buy a puppy so that he could take over your house, but in order for a puppy to grow into a stable, well-adjusted dog, he has to feel comfortable in his surroundings. Remember, he is leaving the warmth and security of his mother and littermates, as well as the familiarity of the only place he has ever known, so it is important to make his transition

**CRATE TRAINING TIPS**
During crate training, you should partition off the section of the crate in which the pup stays. If he is given too big an area, this will hinder your training efforts. Crate training is based on the fact that a dog does not like to soil his sleeping quarters, so it is ineffective to keep a pup in a crate that is so big that he can eliminate in one end and get far enough away from it to sleep. Also, you want to make the crate den-like for the pup. Blankets and a favourite toy will make the crate cosy for the small pup; as he grows, you may want to evict some of his 'roommates' to make more room.

It will take some coaxing at first, but be patient. Given some time to get used to it, your pup will adapt to his new home-within-a-home quite nicely.

as easy as possible. By preparing a place in your home for the puppy, you are making him feel as welcome as possible in a strange new place. It should not take him long to get used to it, but the sudden shock of being transplanted is somewhat traumatic for a young pup. Imagine how a small child would feel in the same situation—that is how your puppy must be feeling. It is up to you to reassure him and to let him know, 'Little chap, you are going to like it here!'

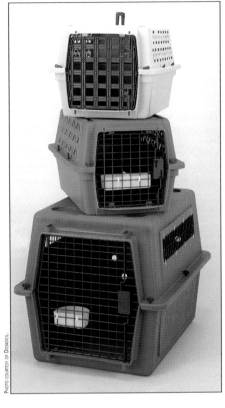

Your local pet shop will have a large array of crates from which you can choose the one which best suits your needs.

## WHAT YOU SHOULD BUY

### CRATE
To someone unfamiliar with the use of crates in dog training, it may seem like punishment to shut a dog in a crate, but this is not the case at all. Although all breeders do not advocate crate training, more and more breeders and trainers are recommending crates as preferred tools for show puppies as well as pet puppies. Crates are not cruel—crates have many humane and highly effective uses in dog care and training. For example, crate training is a very popular and very successful housebreaking method. A crate can keep your dog safe during travel and, perhaps most importantly, a crate provides your dog with a place of his own in your home. It serves as a 'doggie bedroom' of sorts—

your Field Spaniel can curl up in his crate when he wants to sleep or when he just needs a break. Many dogs sleep in their crates overnight. With soft bedding and his favourite toy, a crate becomes a cosy pseudo-den for your dog. Like his ancestors, he too will seek out the comfort and retreat of a den—you just happen to be providing him with something a little more luxurious than what his early ancestors enjoyed.

As far as purchasing a crate, the type that you buy is up to

## TOYS, TOYS, TOYS!

With a big variety of dog toys available, and so many that look like they would be a lot of fun for a dog, be careful in your selection. It is amazing what a set of puppy teeth can do to an innocent-looking toy, so, obviously, safety is a major consideration. Be sure to choose the most durable products that you can find. Hard nylon bones and toys are a safe bet, and many of them are offered in different scents and flavours that will be sure to capture your dog's attention. It is always fun to play a game of catch with your dog, and there are balls and flying discs that are specially made to withstand dog teeth.

PHOTO COURTESY OF MIKKI PET PRODUCTS

you. It will most likely be one of the two most popular types: wire or fibreglass. There are advantages and disadvantages to each type. For example, a wire crate is more open, allowing the air to flow through and affording the dog a view of what is going on around him while a fibreglass crate is sturdier. Both can double as travel crates, providing protection for the dog. The size of the crate is another thing to consider. Puppies do not stay puppies forever—in fact, sometimes it seems as if they grow right before your eyes. It is best to get a crate that will accommodate your dog both as a pup and at full size. A medium-size crate will be necessary for a fully-grown Field Spaniel, perhaps a slightly larger one is necessary for a fully-grown male.

### BEDDING

Veterinary bedding in the dog's crate will help the dog feel more at home and you may also like to pop in a small blanket. This will take the place of the leaves, twigs, etc., that the pup would use in the wild to make a den; the pup can make his own 'burrow' in the crate. Although your pup is far removed from his den-making ancestors, the denning instinct is still a part of his genetic makeup. Second, until you take your pup home, he has been sleeping amidst the warmth of his mother and litter-mates, and while a blanket is not the same as a warm, breathing body, it still provides heat and something with which to snuggle. You will want to wash your pup's bedding frequently in case he has an 'accident' in his crate, and replace or remove any blanket that becomes ragged and starts to fall apart.

## Toys

Toys are a must for dogs of all ages, especially for curious playful pups. Puppies are the 'children' of the dog world, and what child does not love toys? Chew toys provide enjoyment for both dog and owner—your dog will enjoy playing with his favourite toys, while you will enjoy the fact that they distract him from your expensive shoes and leather sofa. Puppies love to chew; in fact, chewing is a physical need for pups as they are teething, and everything looks appetising! The full range of your possessions—from old tea towel to Oriental carpet—are fair game in the eyes of a teething pup. Puppies are not all that discerning when it comes to finding something to literally 'sink their teeth into'—everything tastes great!

During teething, the need to chew will escalate as expected with that developmental phenomenon. Field Spaniels who

### PLAY'S THE THING

Teaching the puppy to play with his toys in running and fetching games is an ideal way to help the puppy develop muscle, learn motor skills and bond with you, his owner and master.

He also needs to learn how to inhibit his bite reflex and never to use his teeth on people, forbidden objects and other animals in play. Whenever you play with your puppy, you make the rules. This becomes an important message to your puppy in teaching him that you are the pack leader and control everything he does in life. Once your dog accepts you as his leader, your relationship with him will be cemented for life.

Pet shops usually
stock a wide
assortment of
leads suitable for
your Field
Spaniel.

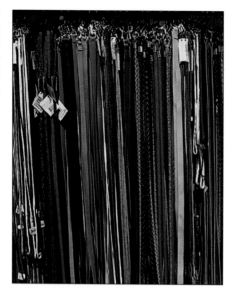

time. The overly excited pup may ingest the stuffing, which not digestible. Similarly, squeaky toys are quite popular, but must be avoided for the Field Spaniel. Perhaps a squeaky toy can be used as an aid in training, but not for free play. If a pup 'disembowels' one of these, the small plastic squeaker inside can be dangerous if swallowed. Monitor the condition of all your pup's toys carefully and get rid of any that have been chewed to the point of becoming potentially dangerous.

are bored are also known to resort to chewing to entertain themselves. It is up to the dog owner to provide appropriate chew items for the dog. An appropriate and generally inexpensive chew item is a raw beef shank (leg) bone available from most butchers in a length of 6 to 8 inches. Rawhide chews, chew hooves and other similar items are not recommended. Rawhide chews quickly become a slimy, sticky mass with an aggressive chewer, whereas chew hooves may break into sharp pieces when chewed. Both have been known to result in digestive ailments, sometimes requiring surgical intervention.

Breeders advise owners to resist stuffed toys, because they can become de-stuffed in no

### LEAD

A nylon lead is probably the best option as it is the most resistant to puppy teeth should your pup take a liking to chewing on his lead. Of course, this is a habit that should be nipped in the bud, but if your pup likes to chew on his lead he has a very slim chance of being able to chew through the strong nylon. Nylon leads are also lightweight, which is good for a young Field Spaniel who is just getting used to the idea of walking on a lead. For everyday walking and safety purposes, the nylon lead is a good choice. As your pup grows up and gets used to walking on the lead, you may want to purchase a flexible lead. These leads allow you to extend the length to give the dog a broader area to explore or to shorten the

# CHOOSE AN APPROPRIATE COLLAR

The BUCKLE COLLAR is the standard collar used for everyday purpose. Be sure that you adjust the buckle on growing puppies. Check it every day. It can become too tight overnight! These collars can be made of leather or nylon. Attach your dog's identification tags to this collar.

The CHOKE COLLAR is the usual collar recommended for training. It is constructed of highly polished steel so that it slides easily through the stainless steel loop. The idea is that the dog controls the pressure around its neck and he will stop pulling if the collar becomes uncomfortable. Never leave a choke collar on your dog when not training.

The HALTER is for a trained dog that has to be restrained to prevent running away, chasing a cat and the like. Considered the most humane of all collars, it is frequently used on smaller dogs for which collars are not comfortable.

Food and water bowls are available in an array of types and sizes. Purchase sturdy bowls for your Field Spaniel.

PHOTO COURTESY OF MIKKI PET PRODUCTS.

length to keep the dog near you. Of course there are special leads for training purposes, and specially made leather harnesses, but these are not necessary for routine walks.

### COLLAR

Your pup should get used to wearing a collar all the time since you will want to attach his ID tags to it. Plus, you have to attach the lead to something! A lightweight nylon collar is a good choice; make sure that it fits snugly enough so that the pup cannot wriggle out of it, but is loose enough so that it will not be uncomfortably tight around the pup's neck. You should be able to fit a finger between the pup and the collar. It may take some time for your pup to get used to wearing the collar, but soon he will not even notice that it is there. Choke collars are made for training, but should only be used by an experienced handler.

### FOOD AND WATER BOWLS

Your pup will need two bowls, one for food and one for water. You may want two sets of bowls, one for inside and one for outside, depending on where the dog will be fed and where he will be spending time. Stainless steel or sturdy plastic bowls are popular choices. Plastic bowls are more chewable. Dogs tend not to chew on the steel variety, which can be sterilised. It is important to buy sturdy bowls since anything is in danger of being chewed by puppy teeth and you do not want your dog to be constantly chewing apart his bowl (for his safety and for your purse!).

### CLEANING SUPPLIES
Until a pup is house-trained you will be doing a lot of cleaning. 'Accidents' will occur, which is acceptable in the beginning because the puppy does not know any better. All you can do is be prepared to clean up any accidents. Old rags, towels, newspapers and a safe disinfectant are good to have on hand.

### BEYOND THE BASICS
The items previously discussed are the bare necessities. You will find out what else you need as you go along—grooming supplies, flea/tick protection, baby gates to partition a room, etc. These things will vary depending on your situation but it is important that you have everything you need to feed and make your Field Spaniel comfortable in his first few days at home.

## PUPPY-PROOFING YOUR HOME
Aside from making sure that your Field Spaniel will be comfortable in your home, you also have to

It is your responsibility to clean up after your Field Spaniel has relieved himself. Your local pet shop will have various aids to assist you in the clean-up task.

make sure that your home is safe for your Field Spaniel. This means taking precautions that your pup will not get into anything he should not get into and that there is nothing within his reach that may harm him should he sniff it, chew it, inspect it, etc. This probably seems obvious since, while you are primarily concerned with your pup's safety, at the same time you do not want your belongings to be ruined. Breakables should be placed out of reach if your dog is to have full run of the house. If he is to be limited to certain places within the house, keep any potentially dangerous items in the 'off-limits' areas. An electrical cord can pose a danger should the puppy decide to taste it—and who is going to convince a pup that it would not make a great chew toy? Cords should be fastened tightly against the wall. If your dog is going to spend time in a crate, make sure that there is nothing near his crate that he can reach if he sticks his curious little nose or paws through the

## PUPPY-PROOFING

Thoroughly puppy-proof your house before bringing your puppy home. Never use roach or rodent poisons in any area accessible to the puppy. Avoid the use of toilet cleaners. Most dogs are born with 'toilet sonar' and will take a drink if the lid is left open. Also keep the rubbish secured and out of reach.

## CHEMICAL TOXINS

Scour your garage for potential puppy dangers. Remove weed killers, pesticides and antifreeze materials. Antifreeze is highly toxic and even a few drops can kill an adult dog. The sweet taste attracts the animal, who will quickly consume it from the floor or curbside.

openings. Just as you would with a child, keep all household cleaners and chemicals where the pup cannot reach them.

It is also important to make sure that the outside of your home is safe. Of course your puppy should never be unsupervised, but a pup let loose in the garden will want to run and explore, and he should be

Provide your Field Spaniel with clean water in his own bowl so that he's not tempted to quench his thirst elsewhere.

## TOXIC PLANTS

Many plants can be toxic to dogs. If you see your dog carrying a piece of vegetation in his mouth, approach him in a quiet, disinterested manner, avoid eye contact, pet him and gradually remove the plant from his mouth. Alternatively, offer him a treat and maybe he'll drop the plant on his own accord. Be sure no toxic plants are growing in your own garden.

granted that freedom. Do not let a fence give you a false sense of security; you would be surprised how crafty (and persistent) a dog can be in working out how to dig under and squeeze his way through small holes, or to jump or climb over a fence. The remedy is to make the fence well embedded into the ground and high enough so that it really is impossible for your dog to get over it (about 3 metres should suffice). Be sure to repair or secure any gaps in the fence. Check the fence periodically to ensure that it is in good shape and make repairs as needed; a very determined pup may return to the same spot to 'work on it' until he is able to get through.

### FIRST TRIP TO THE VET

You have selected your puppy, and your home and family are ready. Now all you have to do is collect your Field Spaniel from

## NATURAL TOXINS

Examine your grass and garden landscaping before bringing your puppy home. Many varieties of plants have leaves, stems or flowers that are toxic if ingested, and you can depend on a curious puppy to investigate them. Ask your vet for information on poisonous plants or research them at your library.

the breeder and the fun begins, right? Well...not so fast. Something else you need to prepare is your pup's first trip to the veterinary surgeon. Perhaps the breeder can recommend someone in the area that specialises in spaniels or hunting breeds, or maybe you know some other Field Spaniel owners who can suggest a good vet. Either way, you should have an appointment arranged for your pup before you pick him up.

Working Field Spaniels enjoy the protection of a weatherproof coat, necessary for the rigours of the hunt.

**TEETHING TIP**
Puppies like soft toys for chewing.
Because they are teething, soft
items like stuffed toys soothe their
aching gums.

The pup's first visit will
consist of an overall examination
to make sure that the pup does
not have any problems that are
not apparent to the eye. The
veterinary surgeon will also set
up a schedule for the pup's
vaccinations; the breeder will
inform you of which ones the
pup has already received and the
vet can continue from there.

**INTRODUCTION
TO THE FAMILY**
Everyone in the house will be
excited about the puppy coming
home and will want to pet him
and play with him, but it is best
to make the introduction low-key
so as not to overwhelm the
puppy. He is apprehensive
already. It is the first time he has
been separated from his mother

and the breeder, and the ride to
your home is likely to be the first
time he has been in a car. The
last thing you want to do is
smother him, as this will only
frighten him further. This is not
to say that human contact is not
extremely necessary at this stage,
because this is the time when a
connection between the pup and
his human family is formed.
Gentle petting and soothing
words should help console him,
as well as just putting him down
and letting him explore on his
own (under your watchful eye, of
course).

The pup may approach the
family members or may busy
himself with exploring for a
while. Gradually, each person
should spend some time with the
pup, one at a time, crouching
down to get as close to the pup's

**THE RIDE HOME**
Taking your dog from the breeder to
your home in a car can be a very
uncomfortable experience for both of
you. The puppy will have been taken
from his warm, friendly, safe environment and brought into a strange new
environment—an environment that
moves! Be prepared for loose bowels,
urination, crying, whining and even
fear biting. With proper love and
encouragement when you arrive
home, the stress of the trip should
quickly disappear.

## FINANCIAL RESPONSIBILITY

Grooming tools, collars, leashes, dog beds and, of course, toys will be an expense to you when you first obtain your pup, and the cost will continue throughout your dog's lifetime. If your puppy damages or destroys your possessions (as most puppies surely will!) or something belonging to a neighbour, you can calculate additional expense. There is also flea and pest control, which every dog owner faces more than once. You must be able to handle the financial responsibility of owning a dog.

perhaps he's even been vaccinated and wormed as well. He's met the family and licked the whole family, including the excited children and the less-than-happy cat. He's explored his area, his new bed, the garden and anywhere else he's been permitted. He's eaten his first meal at home and relieved himself in the proper place. He's heard lots of new sounds,

## FEEDING TIP

You will probably start feeding your pup the same food that he has been getting from the breeder; the breeder should give you a few days' supply to start you off. Although you should not give your pup too many treats, you will want to have puppy treats on hand for coaxing, training, rewards, etc. Be careful, though, as a small pup's calorie requirements are relatively low and a few treats can add up to almost a full day's worth of calories without the required nutrition.

level as possible and letting him sniff their hands and petting him gently. He definitely needs human attention and he needs to be touched—this is how to form an immediate bond. Just remember that the pup is experiencing a lot of things for the first time, at the same time. There are new people, new noises, new smells, and new things to investigate: so be gentle, be affectionate, and be as comforting as you can be.

## PUP'S FIRST NIGHT HOME

You have travelled home with your new charge safely in his crate. He's been to the vet for a thorough check-up; he's been weighed, his papers examined;

**STRESS-FREE**
Some experts in canine health advise that stress during a dog's early years of development can compromise and weaken his immune system, and may trigger the potential for a shortened life expectancy. They emphasise the need for happy and stress-free growing-up years.

smelled new friends and seen more of the outside world than ever before.

That was just the first day! He's worn out and is ready for bed…or so you think!

It's puppy's first night and you are ready to say 'Good night'—keep in mind that this is puppy's first night ever to be sleeping alone. His dam and littermates are no longer at paw's length and he's a bit scared, cold and lonely. Be reassuring to your new family member. This is not the time to spoil him and give in to his inevitable whining.

Puppies whine. They whine to let others know where they are

and hopefully to get company out of it. Place your pup in his new bed or crate in his room and close the door. Mercifully, he may fall asleep without a peep. When the inevitable occurs, ignore the whining: he is fine. Be strong and keep his interest in mind. Do not allow yourself to feel guilty and visit the pup. He will fall asleep eventually.

Many breeders recommend placing a piece of bedding from his former home in his new bed so that he recognises the scent of his littermates. Others still advise placing a hot water bottle in his bed for warmth. This latter may be a good idea provided the pup doesn't attempt to suckle—he'll get good and wet and may not fall asleep so fast.

Puppy's first night can be somewhat stressful for the pup and his new family. Remember that you are setting the tone of nighttime at your house. Unless you want to play with your pup every evening at 10 p.m., midnight and 2 a.m., don't initiate the habit. Your family will thank you, and so will your pup!

## PREVENTING PUPPY PROBLEMS

### SOCIALISATION

Now that you have done all of the preparatory work and have helped your pup get accustomed to his new home and family, it is

## A FORTNIGHT'S GRACE

It will take at least two weeks for your puppy to become accustomed to his new surroundings. Give him lots of love, attention, handling, frequent opportunities to relieve himself, a diet he likes to eat and a place he can call his own.

about time for you to have some fun! Socialising your Field Spaniel pup gives you the opportunity to show off your new friend, and your pup gets to reap the benefits of being an adorable furry creature that people will want to pet and, in general, think is absolutely precious!

Besides getting to know his new family, your puppy should be exposed to other people, animals and situations, but of course he must not come into close contact with dogs you don't know well until his course of injections is fully complete. Socialisation will help him become well adjusted as he grows up and less prone to being timid or fearful of the new things he will encounter. Your pup's socialisation began with the breeder but now it is your responsibility to continue it. The socialisation he receives up until the age of 12 weeks is the most critical, as this is the time when he forms his impressions of the outside world. Be especially careful during the eight-to-ten-week period, also known as the fear period. The interaction he receives during this time should be gentle and reassuring. Lack of socialisation can manifest itself in fear and aggression as the dog grows up. He needs lots of human contact, affection, handling and exposure to other animals.

Once your pup has received his necessary vaccinations, feel free to take him out and about (on his lead, of course). Walk him around the neighbourhood, take him on your daily errands, let people pet him, let him meet other dogs and pets, etc. Puppies

For active Field pups, play is a vital component of every morning, noon and night.

Field Spaniels are intelligent and hard-working dogs. They can be trained to many tasks and they love to retrieve soft articles. The soft articles might remind the dog of the texture of a bird.

## PUPPY PROBLEMS

The majority of problems that are commonly seen in young pups will disappear as your dog gets older. However, how you deal with problems when he is young will determine how he reacts to discipline as an adult dog. It is important to establish who is boss (hopefully it will be you!) right away when you are first bonding with your dog. This bond will set the tone for the rest of your life together.

do not have to try to make friends; there will be no shortage of people who will want to introduce themselves. Just make sure that you carefully supervise each meeting. If the neighbourhood children want to say hello, for example, that is great—children and pups most often make great companions. However, sometimes an excited child can unintentionally handle a pup too roughly, or an overzealous pup can playfully nip a little too hard. You want to make socialisation experiences positive ones. What a pup learns during this very formative stage will affect his attitude toward future encounters. You want your dog to be comfortable around everyone. A pup that has a bad experience with a child may grow up to be a dog that is shy around or aggressive toward children.

### CONSISTENCY IN TRAINING

Dogs, being pack animals, naturally need a leader, or else they try to establish dominance in their packs. When you welcome a dog into your family, the choice of who becomes the leader and who becomes the 'pack' is entirely up to you! Your pup's intuitive quest for dominance, coupled with the fact that it is nearly impossible to look at an adorable Field Spaniel pup with his 'puppy-dog' eyes and not cave in, give the pup almost an unfair advantage in getting the upper hand! A pup will definitely test the waters to see what he can and cannot do. Do not give in to those pleading eyes—stand your ground when it comes to disciplining the pup and make sure that all family members do the same. It will only confuse the pup when Mother tells him to get off the

## SOCIALISATION

Thorough socialisation includes not only meeting new people but also being introduced to new experiences such as riding in the car, having his coat brushed, hearing the television, walking in a crowd—the list is endless. The more your pup experiences, and the more positive the experiences are, the less of a shock and the less frightening it will be for your pup to encounter new things.

Early training of
the Field Spaniel
reinforces his
acceptance of
you as his
all-knowing,
loving leader.

sofa when he is used to sitting up there with Father to watch the nightly news. Avoid discrepancies by having all members of the household decide on the rules before the pup even comes home…and be consistent in enforcing them! Early training shapes the dog's personality, so you cannot be unclear in what you expect.

## COMMON PUPPY PROBLEMS

The best way to prevent puppy problems is to be proactive in stopping an undesirable behaviour as soon as it starts. The old saying 'You can't teach an old dog new tricks' does not necessarily hold true, but it is true that it is much easier to discourage bad behaviour in a young developing pup than to wait until the pup's bad

behaviour becomes the adult dog's bad habit. There are some problems that are especially prevalent in puppies as they develop.

### NIPPING

As puppies start to teethe, they feel the need to sink their teeth into anything available…unfortunately that includes your fingers, arms, hair and toes. You may find this behaviour cute for the first five seconds…until you feel just how sharp those puppy teeth are. This is something you want to discourage immediately and consistently with a firm 'No!' (or whatever number of firm 'No's' it takes for him to understand that you mean business). Then replace your finger with an appropriate chew toy. While this behaviour is merely annoying when the dog is young, it can become dangerous as your Field Spaniel's adult teeth grow in and his jaws develop, and he continues to think it is okay to gnaw on human appendages. Your Field Spaniel does not mean any harm with a friendly nip, but he also does not know his own strength.

### CRYING/WHINING

Your pup will often cry, whine, whimper, howl or make some type of commotion when he is left alone. This is basically his way of calling out for attention to make sure that you know he is there and that you have not forgotten about him. He feels insecure when he is left alone, when you are out of the house and he is in his crate or when you are in another part of the house and he cannot see you. The noise he is making is an expression of the anxiety he feels at being alone, so he needs to be taught that being alone is okay. You are not actually training the dog to stop making noise, you are training him to feel comfortable when he is alone and thus removing the need for him to make the noise. This is where the crate with cosy bedding and a toy comes in handy. You want to know that he is safe when you are not there to supervise, and you know that he will be safe in his crate rather than roaming freely about the house. In order for the pup to stay in his crate without making a fuss, he needs to be comfortable in his crate. On that note, it is extremely important that the crate is never used as a form of punishment, or the pup will have a negative association with the crate.

Accustom the pup to the crate in short, gradually increasing time intervals in which you put him in the crate, maybe with a treat, and stay in the room with him. If he cries or makes a fuss, do not go to him, but stay in his sight. Gradually he will realise that staying in his crate is all right without your help, and it will not be so traumatic for him when you are not around. You may want to leave the radio on softly when you leave the house; the sound of human voices may be comforting to him.

## CHEWING TIPS

Chewing goes hand in hand with nipping in the sense that a teething puppy is always looking for a way to soothe his aching gums. In this case, instead of chewing on you, he may have taken a liking to your favourite shoe or something else which he should not be chewing. Again, realise that this is a normal canine behaviour that does not need to be discouraged, only redirected. Your pup just needs to be taught what is acceptable to chew on and what is off limits. Consistently tell him NO when you catch him chewing on something forbidden and give him a chew toy. Conversely, praise him when you catch him chewing on something appropriate. In this way you are discouraging the inappropriate behaviour and reinforcing the desired behaviour. The puppy chewing should stop after his adult teeth have come in, but an adult dog continues to chew for various reasons—perhaps because he is bored, perhaps to relieve tension or perhaps he just likes to chew. That is why it is important to redirect his chewing when he is still young.

**FEEDING PUPS AND ADULTS**

Today the choices of food for your Field Spaniel are many and varied. There are simply dozens of brands of food in all sorts of flavours and textures, ranging from puppy diets to those for seniors. There are even hypoallergenic and low-calorie diets available. Because your Field Spaniel's food has a bearing on coat, health and temperament, it is essential that the most suitable diet is selected for a Field Spaniel of his age. It is fair to say, however, that even experienced owners can be perplexed by the enormous range of foods available. Only understanding what is best for your dog will help you reach a valued decision.

Dog foods are produced in three basic types: dried, semi-moist and tinned. Dried foods are useful for the cost-conscious for overall they tend to be less expensive than semi-moist or tinned. They also contain the least fat and the most preservatives. In general, tinned foods are made up of 60–70 percent water, while semi-moist ones often contain so much sugar that they are perhaps the least preferred by owners, even though their dogs seem to like them.

Vets often recommend that puppies be maintained on a food formulated for puppies until one year of age. This is not ideal for Field Spaniels. Food formulated specifically for puppies often encourages a rate of growth in body mass (weight) that outpaces the strength of musculature and other soft-tissue support structures. The result is that the front assembly of the dog suffers. Feed a good-quality adult dog food. The Field Spaniel puppy should be lean. Like the gawky human adolescent, the appear-

**TEST FOR PROPER DIET**
A good test for proper diet is the colour, odour and firmness of your dog's stool. A healthy dog usually produces three semi-hard stools per day. The stools should have no unpleasant odour. They should be the same colour from excretion to excretion.

ance should portend that there is much more to come as the frame slowly fills out with maturity.

Many Field Spaniel owners have had considerable success with natural diets for their companions following the recommendations of any one of several reputable authors to assure that the diet is balanced. Some fanciers also believe strongly in using dog dishes that are raised off the floor. Bowl stands are available from most well-stocked pet shops. These stands are thought to be beneficial in providing a more natural feeding position as well as to make the puppy 'stretch' up and avoid bearing down on the front pasterns. It is always wise to consult the breeder of your puppy about specific feeding practices.

## SENIOR DIETS

As dogs get older, their metabolism changes. The older dog usually exercises less, moves more slowly and sleeps more. This change in lifestyle and physiological performance requires a change in diet. Since these changes take place slowly, they might not be recognisable. What is easily recognisable is weight gain. By continuing to feed your dog an adult-maintenance diet when it is slowing down metabolically, your dog will gain weight. Obesity in an

## FOOD PREFERENCE

Selecting the best dried dog food is difficult. There is no majority consensus among veterinary scientists as to the value of nutrient analyses (protein, fat, fibre, moisture, ash, cholesterol, minerals, etc.). All agree that feeding trials are what matter, but you also have to consider the individual dog. The dog's weight, age and activity level, and what pleases his taste, all must be considered. It is probably best to take the advice of your veterinary surgeon. Every dog's dietary requirements vary, even during the lifetime of a particular dog.

If your dog is fed a good dried food, it does not require supplements of meat or vegetables. Dogs do appreciate a little variety in their diets, so you may choose to stay with the same brand but vary the flavour. Alternatively, you may wish to add a little flavoured stock to give a difference to the taste.

**FEEDING TIP**
You must store your dried dog food carefully. Open packages of dog food quickly lose their vitamin value, usually within 90 days of being opened. Mould spores and vermin could also contaminate the food.

older dog compounds the health problems that already accompany old age.

The shift, if any, from adult to senior dog food should be made based on the needs of the individual animal rather than according to age. Senior Fields may often continue to be fed regular adult dog food with no ill effects. Others, particularly those who are less active or with weight-control problems, may do better on a senior food that has fewer calories per cup dried

weight. For seniors with specific medical problems, special diets may be needed.

**WATER**
Just as your dog needs proper nutrition from his food, water is

**SUPPLEMENTING YOUR FIELD SPANIEL'S DIET**
While excessive supplementation is not recommended, there are some supplements commonly used by Field Spaniel fanciers. Among these are:
   **Kelp:** a supplement to enhance overall immune system function and improve coat that is used by a number of fanciers.
   **Vitamin C:** this water-soluble vitamin is often used during major growth phases, typically until the puppy reaches two years of age.
   **Omega fatty-acid supplements:** these oils are often useful, particularly with liver-colour coats, which tend to be somewhat drier and less glossy than the black haircoat.

## DRINK, DRANK, DRUNK— MAKE IT A DOUBLE

In both humans and dogs, as well as most living organisms, water forms the major part of nearly every body tissue. Naturally, we take water for granted, but without it, life as we know it would cease.

For dogs, water is needed to keep their bodies functioning biochemically. Additionally, water is needed to replace the water lost while panting. Unlike humans who are able to sweat to dissipate heat, dogs must pant to cool down, thereby losing the vital water from their bodies needed to regulate their body temperatures. Humans lose electrolyte-containing products and other body-fluid components through sweating; dogs do not lose anything except water.

Water is essential always, but especially so when the weather is hot or humid or when your dog is exercising or working vigorously.

an essential 'nutrient' as well. Water keeps the dog's body properly hydrated and promotes

## NURSING PUPPIES

Puppies instinctively want to suck milk from their mother's teats and a normal puppy will exhibit this behaviour from just a few moments following birth. If puppies do not attempt to suckle within the first half-hour or so, the breeder necessarily encourages them to do so by placing them on the nipples, having selected ones with plenty of milk. This early milk supply is important in providing colostrum to protect the puppies during the first eight to ten weeks of their lives. Although a mother's milk is much better than any milk formula, despite there being some excellent ones available, if the puppies do not feed, the breeder will have to feed them himself. For those with less experience, advice from a veterinary surgeon is important so that not only the right quantity of milk but also that of correct quality is fed, at suitably frequent intervals, usually every two hours during the first few days of life.

Puppies should be allowed to nurse from their mothers for about the first six weeks, although from the third or fourth week the breeder should begin to introduce small portions of suitable solid food. Most breeders like to introduce alternate milk and meat meals initially, building up to weaning time.

# WHAT ARE YOU FEEDING YOUR DOG?

Read the label on your dog food. Many dog foods only advise what 50–55% of the contents are, leaving the other 45% in doubt.

Calcium 1.3%
Fatty Acids 1.6%
Crude Fibre 4.6%
Moisture 11%
Crude Fat 14%
Crude Protein 22%
**45.5% ? ? ?**

normal function of the body's systems. During house-training it is necessary to keep an eye on how much water your Field Spaniel is drinking, but once he is reliably trained he should have access to clean fresh water at all times, especially if you feed dried food. Make certain that the dog's water bowl is clean, and change the water often.

## GROOMING
## THE FIELD SPANIEL

While grooming for the show ring has considerable variations from country to country, there are basic grooming regimens that are necessary for the overall health and well-being of the Field Spaniel as well as for the maintenance of the typical appearance. The basic grooming described

### CHANGE IN DIET

As your dog's caretaker, you know the importance of keeping his diet consistent, but sometimes when you run out of food or if you're on holiday, you have to make a change quickly. Some dogs will experience digestive problems, but most will not. If you are planning on changing your dog's menu, do so gradually to ensure that your dog will not have any problems. Over a period of four to five days, slowly add some new food to your dog's old food, increasing the percentage of new food each day.

### 'DOES THIS COLLAR MAKE ME LOOK FAT?'

While humans may obsess about how they look and how trim their bodies are, many people believe that extra weight on their dogs is a good thing. The truth is, pets should not be over- or under-weight, as both can lead to or signal sickness. In order to tell how fit your pet is, run your hands over his ribs. Are his ribs buried under a layer of fat or are they sticking out considerably? If your pet is within his normal weight range, you should be able to feel the ribs easily, but they should not protrude abnormally. If you stand above him, the outline of his body should resemble an hourglass. Some breeds do tend to be leaner while some are a bit stockier, but making sure your dog is the right weight for his breed will certainly contribute to his good health.

here is for the household companion. Grooming for show may require a bit more to learn and the breeder of your dog is often your very best source of information for learning the requirements of show grooming. There are variations in customs for trimming and preparing the dog for the show ring among fanciers in different countries. Basic grooming equipment needed will vary depending on how you want to groom your Field Spaniel.

**DEADLY DECAY**

Did you know that periodontal disease (a condition of the bone and gums surrounding a tooth) can be fatal? Having your dog's teeth and mouth checked yearly can prevent it.

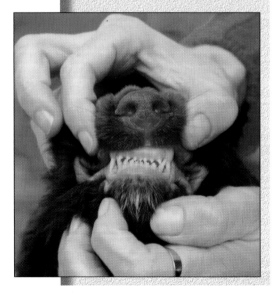

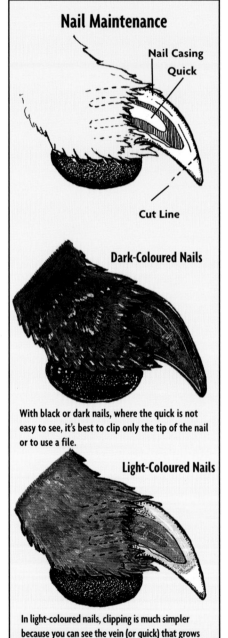

# Nail Maintenance

Nail Casing

Quick

Cut Line

### Dark-Coloured Nails

With black or dark nails, where the quick is not easy to see, it's best to clip only the tip of the nail or to use a file.

### Light-Coloured Nails

In light-coloured nails, clipping is much simpler because you can see the vein (or quick) that grows inside the casing.

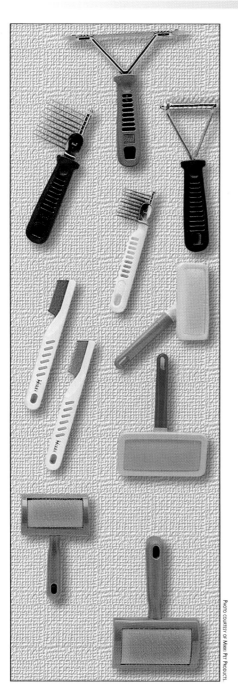

PHOTO COURTESY OF MIKKI PET PRODUCTS.

## GROOMING EQUIPMENT FOR YOUR FIELD SPANIEL

- Nail clipper and nail file or nail grinder
- Styptic powder or liquid
- Ear cleanser, powder or liquid as recommended by your veterinary surgeon or breeder
- Cotton wipes
- Soft toothbrush and canine toothpaste or other dental care products as recommended by the breeder or veterinary surgeon
- Bristle brush (natural bristle style recommended)
- 'Greyhound'-style comb
- Straight shears
- Stripping knife
- Shampoo formulated for canines
- Hand-held blaster
- Electric clipper with 7F blade (optional)
- Thinning shears (optional)
- Grooming spray for daily use (optional)
- Grooming table (optional)
- Coat conditioner for use after bathing (optional)
- SPF-rated sun protection spray for coat (optional)

Your local pet shop will probably have a complete array of grooming tools necessary for the maintenance of your Field Spaniel's coat, nails, ears and eyes.

### CARE OF THE TOENAILS

Field Spaniels generally have tough black toenails and the 'quick' (vascular nail bed) is nearly impossible to see. Nails must be trimmed on a weekly basis, as nails that are too long

**Field Spaniels have tough, black toenails that require regular trimming and maintenance with tools made for dogs' nails.**

may result in improper placement of the foot as the nail hits the floor. A nail clipper is used to clip off the end of the nail, followed by using the nail file to smooth rough edges. Styptic powder is crucial to have nearby as it is all too easy to cut a bit too close. As an alternative, a nail grinder may be used to shorten the nail and provide the same smoothing of the file at the same time. Many dogs dislike nail cutting intensely. This may be avoided by routinely handling the feet at times apart from nail

**PEDICURE TIP**

A dog that spends a lot of time outside on a hard surface, such as cement or pavement, will have his nails naturally worn down and may not need to have them trimmed as often, except maybe in the colder months when he is not outside as much. Regardless, it is best to get your dog accustomed to the nail-trimming procedure at an early age so that he is used to it. Some dogs are especially sensitive about having their feet touched, but if a dog has experienced it since puppyhood, it should not bother him.

**A frequently neglected aspect of grooming dogs is their teeth. Your Field Spaniel's teeth should be brushed at least once per week.**

cutting and introducing the puppy to the regimen at an early age.

### ORAL HEALTH

Routine care of the mouth is important to prevent tooth decay and gum disease. Weekly attention to brushing the teeth is helpful to maintain the teeth in the best possible manner. While providing chew bones is helpful to naturally remove tartar build-up as the dog gnaws, this is often not sufficient. You can purchase a dog toothbrush and paste at your local pet shop or from your vet.

### TENDING TO THE EARS

The beautiful ears of the Field Spaniel that frame the face so well and contribute greatly to the soft spaniel expression do require routine care. Ears should be cleaned weekly using cotton

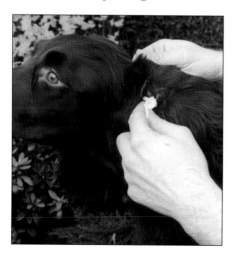

wipes and a powder or liquid cleansing agent as recommended by your veterinary surgeon or breeder. Do not be tempted to use a cotton bud rather than the cotton wipe. It is far too easy to probe too deeply with a bud and cause harm. Routine care of the ear helps prevent ear infections in this breed with pendulous ears as the weight and length of the ear effectively cloak the ear opening, thereby creating an ideal dark, moist environment for infection. It is recommended that the hair around the ear opening be shortened by plucking or by careful use of thinning shears to keep the ear as dry as possible, particularly for Field Spaniels who do a bit of swimming.

Tear stains can be removed with a cotton wipe and tear stain remover available from your local pet shop.

Your Field Spaniel's ears should be cleaned weekly using cotton wipes and a cleansing agent made especially for dogs.

### BATHING YOUR FIELD SPANIEL

The frequency of bathing will depend greatly on the dog's activities as well as the coat of

### NAIL FILING

You can purchase an electric tool to grind down a dog's nails rather than cut them. Some dogs don't seem to mind the electric grinder but will object strongly to nail clippers. Talking it over with your veterinary surgeon will help you make the right choice.

the dog. Some Field Spaniels have coats that are oilier than others and these may begin to become 'doggy' more quickly. Therefore, if your Field Spaniel is a household companion and sleeps on your bed, you may wish to bath your dog up a bit more often! Fields who are shown are often bathed far more frequently, particularly during show season. On the average, a home companion will require bathing no more frequently than

### SOAP IT UP

The use of human soap products like shampoo, bubble bath and hand soap can be damaging to a dog's coat and skin. Human products are too strong; they remove the protective oils coating the dog's hair and skin that make him water-resistant. Use only shampoo made especially for dogs. You may like to use a medicated shampoo, which will help to keep external parasites at bay.

once a month, especially if routine coat care via a thorough brushing is done.

When bathing your Field, cotton used in the outer ear will prevent water from getting into the ear canal. Using tepid water, just warm to the touch,

### BATHING BEAUTY

Once you are sure that the dog is thoroughly rinsed, squeeze the excess water out of his coat with your hand and dry him with a heavy towel. You may choose to use a blaster on his coat or just let it dry naturally. In cold weather, never allow your dog outside with a wet coat.

There are 'dry bath' products on the market, which are sprays and powders intended for spot cleaning, that can be used between regular baths if necessary. They are not substitutes for regular baths, but they are easy to use for touch-ups as they do not require rinsing.

thoroughly wet the dog, beginning at the head and working toward the tail, and from the top of the head to the feet. Using a product designed for dogs, not humans, apply shampoo as directed on the bottle, but avoid the face while doing so to prevent any irritation to the sensitive eyes. The face is easily cleaned using a damp face flannel. There are many different shampoo formulations available, some of which are medicated for use with specific coat and skin problems. The mildest shampoo is often the best to avoid stripping the coat of essential oils, particularly in the liver-coloured coats. After thoroughly lathering the dog, paying attention to leg, belly and ear feathering, thoroughly rinse him with tepid water. A spray device,

Hair on the dog's hind legs is often shortened from hock to ground.

styling your own hair without tangles, so it works with Field Spaniel feathering. Following rinsing, it is essential to dry the haircoat. A hand-held blaster set on 'low' works quite well. Take care to direct the airflow away from the face and to maintain a

Untrimmed (left) versus trimmed (right) hind legs.

such as used for showering, makes the job of rinsing the dog much easier to accomplish. It is essential that all traces of shampoo be removed, as leaving any shampoo in the coat will attract dirt as well as potentially irritate the skin.

It is helpful to apply a coat conditioner during final brushing after drying the dog. Just as a conditioning rinse is helpful to

The Field Spaniel head trimmed on only one side to show the difference before and after trimming.

The use of thinning shears in blending the hair on the neck area.

Shears are used carefully to shorten hair around the ear opening.

safe distance between the dryer and the dog. When dry, use the bristle brush for the body coat and the comb to smooth out feathering.

### BRUSHING AND COMBING

Many Field Spaniels really enjoy spending time with their owners and the brush and comb! After all, it is a time when your dog has your undivided attention, and regular grooming can be very relaxing for both you and your dog. On at least a weekly basis, use the bristle brush, starting at the top of the skull and working toward the tail, always going with the lay of the hair. Avoid

brushing the facial area; use a barely damp face flannel to groom this area, again always following the lay of the hair. Brushing removes dead hair and, with regular application, you will see far less moulting in the form of fluff-balls of dog hair drifting into corners! A conditioning grooming spray may be used during brushing; this is particularly helpful for dogs who will be shown in the conformation ring as it helps prevent coat breakage.

Following brushing, use the comb for feathering on the ears, legs and belly area. Gently work out any tangles that might be present to avoid any discomfort

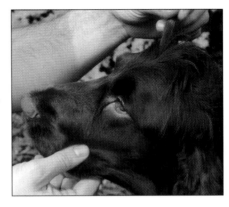

Hand plucking requires time to learn and practice to master.

The tail needs attention, too. The grooming tool used here is the thinning shears.

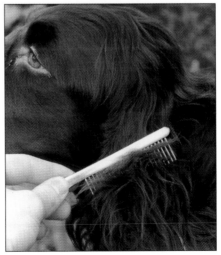

Following brushing, use the comb for feathering on the ears.

(centre) A Field Spaniel puppy properly trimmed. Adults, of course, require more grooming and coat care than puppies.

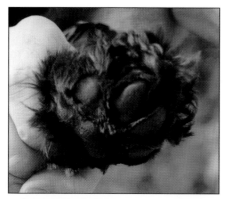

The un-trimmed foot of a Field Spaniel.

Excess hair should be scissored off.

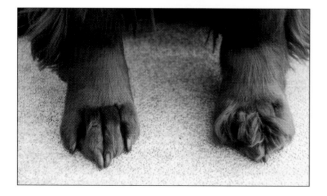

Compare the trimmed and un-trimmed feet.

to your dog. If needed, depending on how much time your Field Spaniel spends outdoors, a sunscreen spray is helpful to apply as a final mist to prevent bleaching of the coat, which is particularly a problem for the liver coat colour.

**TRIMMING THE FIELD'S COAT**
Neatening up the haircoat is helpful to maintain typical Field Spaniel appearance, whether the dog is a household companion or show dog. Trimming, even for the show ring, should only enhance the natural appearance of the dog. The choice of tools to use for trimming the haircoat varies considerably among fanciers. It is safe to say that the stripping knife is utilised worldwide to remove dead coat as well as to blend coat or remove excessive length, while the straight shears are used to shorten the hair on the back of the rear leg from hock to ground. The straight shear should also be carefully used to trim hair from the footpads so that the dog is not walking on hair, thereby losing the natural traction supplied by the pad.

In general, the hair on the upper one-third of the outer ear is shortened to enhance the appearance of the set of the ear, allowing the ear to gracefully frame the face. This may be accomplished by use of the stripping knife or thinning shears, used to both shorten as necessary and blend the hair to lay flat and create a gradual transition of the hair from skull to ear to neck. Hair from the lower jaw (an area about two finger-breadths above the prosternum of the chest) may also be shortened with a stripping knife to enhance the neckline of the dog. Again, the key is to remove just enough hair to neaten the appearance and blend well into the longer body coat.

Excessive facial hair may be carefully stripped by use of a small stripping knife created expressly for that purpose. Though in the United States and Canada, an electric clipper with 7F blade is often used for the ear, face and throat, this is not considered an ideal way to shorten the hair in the UK and many other countries where use of the electric clipper is particularly discouraged. Clipping may create a somewhat more artificial appearance and is considered by some to be a culprit in premature greying of the clipped hair. In all countries, the stripping knife is the preferred tool to use on body coat to remove fuzzy hair as commonly seen on liver-coloured dogs. An electric clipper or thinning shears should never be applied to body coat as this may potentially ruin the proper texture of the coat. As an alterna-

**EXERCISE ALERT!**
You should be careful where you exercise your dog. Many countryside areas have been sprayed with chemicals that are highly toxic to both dogs and humans. Never allow your dog to eat grass or drink from puddles on either public or private grounds, as the run-off water may contain chemicals from sprays and herbicides.

tive to the stripping knife, hand plucking of the body coat may also be done. Though this is very time-consuming and can take a bit of practice to master, the end result does produce the best possible coat texture.

**EXERCISE**
The Field Spaniel's exercise needs vary greatly among

**EXERCISE CAUTION**
Never tie a dog out to a post or tree,
thinking that you are giving him
exercise. This will only serve to
increase aggression in the dog; in
some circumstances, tying the dog
out can make him mean.

individuals. Field Spaniels from
lines bred for not only conformation but working ability (hunting,
obedience, agility, tracking) will
typically need more exercise than
those from lines bred primarily
for the conformation show ring
with less emphasis on performance. On the average, a couple of
brisk 15- to 20-minute walks and
a daily session throwing a tennis
ball or retrieving a bumper in the
garden are recommended.
Creating a safe place for a Field
Spaniel puppy to play freely,
such as a fenced garden, is
helpful to allow the puppy to
exercise to the amount that the
puppy requires. All Field

Spaniels need quality exercise
that includes interaction and
playtime with their human
companions; this is not a breed
that will be content to be
relegated to the garden without
human interaction.

**HEAT STROKE**
Never leave your dog alone in the car.
In hot weather, your dog can die from
the high temperature inside a closed
vehicle; even a car parked in the shade
can heat up very quickly. Leaving the
window open is dangerous as well
since the dog can hurt himself trying
to get out.

**ON THE ROAD**
If you are going on a long motor
trip with your dog, be sure the
hotels are dog-friendly. Many
hotels do not accept dogs. Also
take along some ice that can be
thawed and offered to your dog
if he becomes overheated. Most
dogs like to lick ice.

**If you travel with your Field Spaniel fairly regularly, you can have your car outfitted to protect both of you when driving or when resting.**

**SAFETY TIP**

The most extensive travel you do with your dog may be limited to trips to the veterinary surgeon's office—or you may decide to bring him along for long distances when the family goes on holiday. Whichever the case, it is important to consider your dog's safety while travelling.

## TRAVELLING WITH YOUR DOG

### CAR TRAVEL

You should accustom your Field Spaniel to riding in a car at an early age. You may or may not take him in the car often, but at the very least he will need to go to the vet and you do not want these trips to be traumatic for the dog or troublesome for you. The safest way for a dog to ride in the car is in his crate. If he uses a crate in the house, you can use the same crate for travel.

Put the pup in the crate and see how he reacts. If he seems uneasy, you can have a passenger hold him on his lap while you drive. Another option is a specially made safety harness for dogs, which straps the dog in much like a seat belt. Do not let the dog roam loose in the vehicle—this is very dangerous! If you should stop short, your dog can be thrown and injured. If the dog starts climbing on you and pestering you while you are driving, you will not be able to concentrate on the road. It is an unsafe situation for everyone—human and canine.

For long trips, be prepared to stop to let the dog relieve

**TRAVEL TIP**

When travelling, never let your dog off-lead in a strange area. Your dog could run away out of fear, decide to chase a passing squirrel or cat or simply want to stretch his legs without restriction—if any of these happen, you might never see your canine friend again.

## MOTION SICKNESS

*If life is a motorway...*your dog may not want to come along for the ride! Some dogs experience motion sickness in cars that leads to excessive salivation and even vomiting. In most cases, your dog will fare better in the familiar, safe confines of his crate. To desensitise your dog, try going on several short jaunts before trying a long trip. If your dog experiences distress when riding in the vehicle, drive with him only when absolutely necessary, and do not feed him or give him water before you go.

himself. Take with you whatever you need to clean up after him, including some paper kitchen towels and perhaps some old towelling for use should he have an accident in the car or suffer from travel sickness.

**A wire crate can be used in your car or home but it is usually unacceptable for shipping your dog by bus, train or plane.**

### AIR TRAVEL

While it is possible to take a dog on a flight within Britain, this is fairly unusual and advance permission is always required. The dog will be required to travel in a fibreglass crate and you should always check in advance with the airline regarding specific requirements. To help the dog be at ease, put one of his favourite toys in the crate with him. Do not feed the dog for at least six hours before the trip to minimise his need to relieve himself. However, certain regulations specify that water must always be made available to the dog in the crate.

Make sure your dog is properly identified and that your

find out that they do not allow dogs. Also, you do not want to reserve a place for your family without confirming that you are travelling with a dog because if it is against their policy you may not have a place to stay.

Alternatively, if you are travelling and choose not to bring your Field Spaniel, you will have to make arrangements for him while you are away. Some

You should select a suitable boarding kennel before you actually need one so that you are prepared in advance.

contact information appears on his ID tags and on his crate. Animals travel in a different area of the plane than human passengers so every rule must be strictly followed so as to prevent the risk of getting separated from your dog.

### BOARDING

So you want to take a family holiday—and you want to include all members of the family. You would probably make arrangements for accommodation ahead of time anyway, but this is especially important when travelling with a dog. You do not want to make an overnight stop at the only place around for miles and

**LET THE SUN SHINE**
Your dog needs daily sunshine for the same reason people do. Pets kept inside homes with curtains drawn against the sun suffer 'SAD' (Seasonal Affected Disorder) to the same degree as humans. We now know that sunlight must enter the iris and thus progress to the pineal gland to regulate the body's hormonal system. When we live and work in artificial light, both circadian rhythms and hormone balances are disturbed.

For safety's sake, your Field Spaniel should never be without his identification tag on a light collar.

options are to take him to a neighbour's house to stay while you are gone, to have a trusted neighbour pop in often or stay at your house, or bring your dog to a reputable boarding kennel. If you choose to board him at a kennel, you should visit in advance to see the facilities provided, how clean they are and where the dogs are kept. Talk to some of the employees and see how they treat the dogs—do they spend time with the dogs, play with them, exercise them, etc.? Also find out the kennel's policy on vaccinations and what they require. This is for all of the dogs' safety, since when dogs are kept together, there is a risk of diseases being passed from dog to dog.

## IDENTIFICATION

Your Field Spaniel is your valued companion and friend. That is why you always keep a close eye on him and you have made sure that he cannot escape from the garden or wriggle out of his collar

### ID TAGS

If your dog gets lost, he is not able to ask for directions home. Identification tags fastened to the collar give important information— the dog's name, the owner's name, the owner's address and a telephone number where the owner can be reached. This makes it easy for whomever finds the dog to contact the owner and arrange to have the dog returned. An added advantage is that a person will be more likely to approach a lost dog who has ID tags on his collar; it tells the person that this is somebody's pet rather than a stray. This is the easiest and fastest method of identification, provided that the tags stay on the collar and the collar stays on the dog.

and run away from you. However, accidents can happen and there may come a time when your dog unexpectedly gets separated from you. If this unfortunate event should occur, the first thing on your mind will be finding him. Proper identification, including

### DID YOU KNOW?

You have a valuable dog. If the dog is lost or stolen, you would undoubtedly become extremely upset. Likewise, if you encounter a lost dog, notify the police or the local animal shelter.

## IDENTITY CRISIS!

Surely you know the importance of good nutrition, good training and a good home, but are you aware of the importance of identification tags for your dog? If your dog ran away or got lost, ID tags on your pet's collar would provide crucial information such as the dog's name and your name and contact information, making it possible that your dog would soon be returned. Every morning before taking your dog out, make sure his collar and tags are present and securely fastened.

an ID tag, a tattoo and possibly a microchip, will increase the chances of his being returned to you safely and quickly.

## VACCINATIONS

For international travel you will have to make arrangements well in advance (perhaps months), as countries' regulations pertaining to bringing in animals differ. There may be special health certificates and/or vaccinations that your dog will need before taking the trip; sometimes this has to be done within a certain time frame. In rabies-free countries, you will need to bring proof of the dog's rabies vaccination and there may be a quarantine period upon arrival.

## IDENTIFICATION OPTIONS

As puppies become more and more expensive, especially those puppies of high quality for showing and/or breeding, they have a greater chance of being stolen. The usual collar dog tag is, of course, easily removed. But there are two more permanent techniques that have become widely used for identification.

The puppy microchip implantation involves the injection of a small microchip, about the size of a corn kernel, under the skin of the dog. If your dog shows up at a clinic or shelter, or is offered for resale under less than savoury circumstances, it can be positively identified by the microchip. The microchip is scanned, and a registry quickly identifies you as the owner. This is not only protection against theft, but should the dog run away or go chasing a squirrel and become lost, you have a fair chance of his being returned to you.

Tattooing is done on various parts of the dog, from his belly to his cheeks. The number tattooed can be your telephone number or any other number that you can easily memorise. When professional dog thieves see a tattooed dog, they usually lose interest. Both microchipping and tattooing can be done at your local veterinary clinic. For the safety of our dogs, no laboratory facility or dog broker will accept a tattooed dog as stock.

# Training Your

# FIELD SPANIEL

**REAP THE REWARDS**
If you start with a normal, healthy dog and give him time, patience and some carefully executed lessons, you will reap the rewards of that training for the life of the dog. And what a life it will be! The two of you will find immeasurable pleasure in the companionship you have built together with love, respect and understanding.

Living with an untrained dog is a lot like owning a piano that you do not know how to play—it is a nice object to look at but it does not do much more than that to bring you pleasure. Now try taking piano lessons and suddenly the piano comes alive and brings forth magical sounds and rhythms that set your heart singing and your body swaying.

The same is true with your Field Spaniel. Any dog is a big responsibility and if not trained sensibly may develop unacceptable behaviour that annoys you or could even cause family friction.

To train your Field Spaniel, you may like to enrol in an obedience class. Teach him good manners as you learn how and why he behaves the way he does. Find out how to communicate with your dog and how to recognise and understand his communications with you. Suddenly the dog takes on a new role in your life—he is clever, interesting, well-behaved and fun to be with. He demonstrates his bond of devotion to you daily. In

## THE HAND THAT FEEDS

To a dog's way of thinking, your hands are like his mouth in terms of a defence mechanism. If you squeeze him too tightly, he might just bite you because that would be his normal response. This is not aggressive biting and, although all biting should be discouraged, you need the discipline in learning how to handle your dog.

Even a trained adult dog should practise the basic commands on a regular basis. Fields thrive on reinforcement and praise.

other words, your Field Spaniel does wonders for your ego because he constantly reminds you that you are not only his leader, you are his hero!

Those involved with teaching dog obedience and counselling owners about their dogs' behaviour have discovered some interesting facts about dog ownership. For example, training dogs when they are puppies results in the highest rate of success in developing well-

## PARENTAL GUIDANCE

Training a dog is a life experience. Many parents admit that much of what they know about raising children they learned from caring for their dogs. Dogs respond to love, fairness and guidance, just as children do. Become a good dog owner and you may become an even better parent.

mannered and well-adjusted adult dogs. Training an older dog, from six months to six years of age, can produce almost equal results providing that the owner accepts the dog's slower rate of learning capability and is willing to work patiently to help the dog succeed at developing to his fullest potential. Unfortunately, many owners of untrained adult dogs lack the patience factor, so they do not persist until their dogs are successful at learning particular behaviours.

Training a puppy aged 10 to 16 weeks (20 weeks at the most) is like working with a dry sponge in a pool of water. The pup soaks up whatever you show him and constantly looks for more things to do and learn. At this early age, his body is not yet producing hormones, and therein lies the reason for such a high rate of success. Without hormones, he is focused on his owners and not particularly interested in investigating other places, dogs, people, etc. You are his leader: his provider of food, water, shelter and security. He latches onto you and wants to stay close. He will usually follow you from room to room, will not let you out of his sight when you are outdoors with him and will respond in like manner to the people and animals you encounter. If you greet a friend warmly, he will be happy to greet the person

## HONOUR AND OBEY

Dogs are the most honourable animals in existence. They consider another species (humans) as their own. They interface with you. You are their leader. Puppies perceive children to be on their level; their actions around small children are different from their behaviour around their adult masters.

as well. If, however, you are hesitant, even anxious, about the approach of a stranger, he will respond accordingly.

Once the puppy begins to produce hormones, his natural curiosity emerges and he begins to investigate the world around him. It is at this time when you may notice that the untrained dog begins to wander away from you and even ignore your commands to stay close. When this behaviour becomes a problem, the owner has two choices: get rid of the dog or train him. It is strongly urged that you choose the latter option.

There are usually classes within a reasonable distance from the owner's home, but you can also do a lot to train your dog yourself. Sometimes there are classes available but the tuition is too costly. Whatever the circumstances, the solution to the problem of lack of lesson availability lies within the pages of this book.

## MEALTIME

Mealtime should be a peaceful time for your puppy. Do not put his food and water bowls in a high-traffic area in the house. For example, give him his own little corner of the kitchen where he can eat undisturbed and where he will not be underfoot. Do not allow small children or other family members to disturb the pup when he is eating.

This chapter is devoted to helping you train your Field Spaniel at home. If the recommended procedures are followed faithfully, you may expect positive results that will prove rewarding both to you and your dog.

Whether your new charge is a puppy or a mature adult, the methods of teaching and the techniques we use in training basic behaviours are the same. After all, no dog, whether puppy or adult, likes harsh or inhumane methods. All creatures, however, respond favourably to gentle motivational methods and sincere praise and encouragement. Now let us get started.

## HOUSE-TRAINING

You can train a puppy to relieve itself wherever you choose, but this must be somewhere suitable. You should bear in mind from the outset that when your puppy is old enough to go out in public

**TRAINING TIP**
Dogs will do anything for your attention. If you reward the dog when he is calm and resting, you will develop a well-mannered dog. If, on the other hand, you greet your dog excitedly and encourage him to wrestle with you, the dog will greet you the same way and you will have a hyperactive dog on your hands.

**THINK BEFORE YOU BARK**
Dogs are sensitive to their masters' moods and emotions. Use your voice wisely when communicating with your dog. Never raise your voice at your dog unless you are angry and trying to correct him. 'Barking' at your dog can become as meaningless as 'dogspeak' is to you. Think before you bark!

places, any canine deposits must be removed at once. You will always have to carry with you a small plastic bag or 'poop-scoop.'

Outdoor training includes such surfaces as grass, soil and cement. Indoor training usually means training your dog to newspaper.

When deciding on the surface and location that you will want

### PAPER CAPER

Never line your pup's sleeping area with newspaper. Puppy litters are usually raised on newspaper and, once in your home, the puppy will immediately associate newspaper with voiding. Never put newspaper on any floor while house-training, as this will only confuse the puppy. If you are paper-training him, use paper in his designated relief area ONLY. Finally, restrict water intake after evening meals. Offer a few licks at a time—never let a young puppy gulp water after meals.

your Field Spaniel to use, be sure it is going to be permanent. Training your dog to grass and then changing your mind two months later is extremely difficult for both dog and owner.

Next, choose the command you will use each and every time you want your puppy to void. 'Hurry up' and 'Toilet' are

examples of commands commonly used by dog owners.

Get in the habit of giving the puppy your chosen relief command before you take him out. That way, when he becomes an adult, you will be able to determine if he wants to go out when you ask him. A confirmation will be signs of interest, wagging his tail, watching you intently, going to the door, etc.

### PUPPY'S NEEDS

Puppy needs to relieve himself after play periods, after each meal, after he has been sleeping and at any time he indicates that he is looking for a place to urinate or defecate.

The urinary and intestinal tract muscles of very young puppies are not fully developed. Therefore, like human babies, puppies need to relieve themselves frequently.

Take your puppy out often—every hour for an eight-week-old, for example, and always immediately after sleeping and eating. The older the puppy, the less often he will need to relieve

### ATTENTION!

Your dog is actually training you at the same time you are training him. Dogs do things to get attention. They usually repeat whatever succeeds in getting your attention.

# CANINE DEVELOPMENT SCHEDULE

It is important to understand how and at what age a puppy develops into adulthood. If you are a puppy owner, consult the following Canine Development Schedule to determine the stage of development your puppy is currently experiencing. This knowledge will help you as you work with the puppy in the weeks and months ahead.

| Period | Age | Characteristics |
|---|---|---|
| FIRST TO THIRD | BIRTH TO SEVEN WEEKS | Puppy needs food, sleep and warmth, and responds to simple and gentle touching. Needs mother for security and disciplining. Needs littermates for learning and interacting with other dogs. Pup learns to function within a pack and learns pack order of dominance. Begin socialising with adults and children for short periods. Begins to become aware of its environment. |
| FOURTH | EIGHT TO TWELVE WEEKS | Brain is fully developed. Needs socialising with outside world. Remove from mother and littermates. Needs to change from canine pack to human pack. Human dominance necessary. Fear period occurs between 8 and 12 weeks. Avoid fright and pain. |
| FIFTH | THIRTEEN TO SIXTEEN WEEKS | Training and formal obedience should begin. Less association with other dogs, more with people, places, situations. Period will pass easily if you remember this is pup's change-to-adolescence time. Be firm and fair. Flight instinct prominent. Permissiveness and over-disciplining can do permanent damage. Praise for good behaviour. |
| JUVENILE | FOUR TO EIGHT MONTHS | Another fear period about 7 to 8 months of age. It passes quickly, but be cautious of fright and pain. Sexual maturity reached. Dominant traits established. Dog should understand sit, down, come and stay by now. |

NOTE: THESE ARE APPROXIMATE TIME FRAMES. ALLOW FOR INDIVIDUAL DIFFERENCES IN PUPPIES.

a child loose in a sports arena and telling the child that the place is all his! The sheer enormity of the place would be too much for him to handle.

## COMMAND STANCE

Stand up straight and authoritatively when giving your dog commands. Do not issue commands when lying on the floor or lying on your back on the sofa. If you are on your hands and knees when you give a command, your dog will think you are positioning yourself to play.

### PRACTICE MAKES PERFECT!

• Have training lessons with your dog every day in several short segments—three to five times a day for a few minutes at a time is ideal.

• Do not have long practice sessions. The dog will become easily bored.

• Never practise when you are tired, ill, worried or in an otherwise negative mood. This will transmit to the dog and may have an adverse effect on its performance.

Think fun, short and above all POSITIVE! End each session on a high note, rather than a failed exercise, and make sure to give a lot of praise. Enjoy the training and help your dog enjoy it, too.

himself. Finally, as a mature healthy adult, he will require only three to five relief trips per day.

### HOUSING

Since the types of housing and control you provide for your puppy have a direct relationship on the success of house-training, we consider the various aspects of both before we begin training.

Taking a new puppy home and turning him loose in your house can be compared to turning

## THE GOLDEN RULE

The golden rule of dog training is simple. For each 'question' (command), there is only one correct answer (reaction). One command = one reaction. Keep practising the command until the dog reacts correctly without hesitating. Be repetitive but not monotonous. Dogs get bored just as people do!

A wire crate is good for use inside your home. Do not place the puppy's water bowl in the crate until house-training is complete.

Instead, offer the puppy clearly defined areas where he can play, sleep, eat and live. A room of the house where the family gathers is the most obvious choice. Puppies are social animals and need to feel a part of the pack right from the start. Hearing your voice, watching you while you are doing things and smelling you nearby are all positive reinforcers that he is now a member of your pack. Usually a family room, the kitchen or a nearby adjoining breakfast area is ideal for providing safety and security for both puppy and owner.

Within that room there should be a smaller area that the puppy can call his own. An alcove, a wire or fibreglass dog

crate or a fenced (not boarded!) corner from which he can view the activities of his new family will be fine. The size of the area or crate is the key factor here. The area must be large enough for the puppy to lie down and stretch out as well as stand up without rubbing his head on the top, yet small enough so that he

## THE CLEAN LIFE

By providing sleeping and resting quarters that fit the dog, and offering frequent opportunities to relieve himself outside his quarters, the puppy quickly learns that the outdoors (or the newspaper if you are training him to paper) is the place to go when he needs to urinate or defecate. It also reinforces his innate desire to keep his sleeping quarters clean. This, in turn, helps develop the muscle control that will eventually produce a dog with clean living habits.

Always clean up after your Field Spaniel relieves itself, whether you're in a public place or your own garden.

## SUCCESS IS THE NAME

Success that comes by luck is usually short-lived. Success that comes by well-thought-out proven methods is often more easily achieved and permanent. This is the Success Method. It is designed to give you, the puppy owner, a simple yet proven way to help your puppy develop clean living habits and a feeling of security in his new environment.

cannot relieve himself at one end and sleep at the other without coming into contact with his droppings until fully trained to relieve himself outside.

Dogs are, by nature, clean animals and will not remain close to their relief areas unless forced to do so. In those cases, they then become dirty dogs and usually remain that way for life.

The designated area should contain clean bedding and a toy. Water must always be available, in a non-spill container.

# THE SUCCESS METHOD

**1** Tell the puppy 'Crate time!' and place him in the crate with a small treat (a piece of cheese or half of a biscuit). Let him stay in the crate for five minutes while you are in the same room. Then release him and praise lavishly. Never release him when he is fussing. Wait until he is quiet before you let him out.

**2** Repeat Step 1 several times a day.

**3** The next day, place the puppy in the crate as before. Let him stay there for ten minutes. Do this several times.

**4** Continue building time in five-minute increments until the puppy

stays in his crate for 30 minutes with you in the room. Always take him to his relief area after prolonged periods in his crate.

**5** Now go back to Step 1 and let the puppy stay in his crate for five minutes, this time while you are out of the room.

**6** Once again, build crate time in five-minute increments with you out of the room. When the puppy will stay willingly in his crate (he may even fall asleep!) for 30 minutes with you out of the room, he will be ready to stay in it for several hours at a time.

## *6 Steps to Successful Crate Training*

## HOW MANY TIMES A DAY?

| AGE | RELIEF TRIPS |
| --- | --- |
| To 14 weeks | 10 |
| 14–22 weeks | 8 |
| 22–32 weeks | 6 |
| Adulthood | 4 |
| (dog stops growing) | |

These are estimates, of course, but they are a guide to the MINIMUM opportunities a dog should have each day to relieve itself.

### CONTROL

By control, we mean helping the puppy to create a lifestyle pattern that will be compatible to that of his human pack (YOU!). Just as we guide little children to learn our way of life, we must show the puppy when it is time to play, eat, sleep, exercise and even entertain himself.

Your puppy should always sleep in his crate. He should also learn that, during times of household confusion and excessive human activity such as at breakfast when family members are preparing for the day, he can play by himself in relative safety and comfort in his designated area. Each time you leave the puppy alone, he should understand exactly where he is to stay. Puppies are chewers. They cannot tell the difference between lamp cords, television wires, shoes, table legs, etc. Chewing into a television wire, for example, can be fatal to the puppy while a shorted wire can start a fire in the house.

If the puppy chews on the arm of the chair when he is alone, you will probably discipline him angrily when you get home. Thus, he makes the association that your

### TRAINING RULES

If you want to be successful in training your dog, you have four rules to obey yourself:
1. Develop an understanding of how a dog thinks.
2. Do not blame the dog for lack of communication.
3. Define your dog's personality and act accordingly.
4. Have patience and be consistent.

## HOUSE-TRAINING TIP

Most of all, be consistent. Always take your dog to the same location, always use the same command and always have the dog on lead when he is in his relief area, unless a fenced-in garden is available.

By following the Success Method, your puppy will be completely house-trained by the time his muscle and brain development reach maturity. Keep in mind that small breeds usually mature faster than large breeds, but all puppies should be trained by six months of age.

coming home means he is going to be punished. (He will not remember chewing the chair and is incapable of making the association of the discipline with his naughty deed.)

Other times of excitement, such as family parties, etc., can be fun for the puppy providing he can view the activities from the

## KEEP SMILING

Never train your dog, puppy or adult, when you are angry or in a sour mood. Dogs are very sensitive to human feelings, especially anger, and if your dog senses that you are angry or upset, he will connect your anger with his training and learn to resent or fear his training sessions.

security of his designated area. He is not underfoot and he is not being fed all sorts of titbits that will probably cause him stomach distress, yet he still feels a part of the fun.

### SCHEDULE

A puppy should be taken to his relief area each time he is released from his designated area, after meals, after a play session and when he first awakens in the morning (at age eight weeks, this can mean 5 a.m.!). The puppy will indicate that he's ready 'to go' by circling or sniffing busily—do not misinterpret these signs. For a puppy less than ten weeks of age, a routine of taking him out every hour is necessary. As the puppy grows, he will be able to wait for

Most breeders concur that males, more fixed on their toileting habits, require more patience to house-train than do females.

longer periods of time.

Keep trips to his relief area short. Stay no more than five or six minutes and then return to the house. If he goes during that time, praise him lavishly and take him indoors immediately. If he does not, but he has an accident when you go back indoors, pick him up immediately, say 'No! No!' and return to his relief area. Wait a few minutes, then return to the house again. Never hit a puppy or rub his face in urine or excrement when he has had an accident!

Once indoors, put the puppy in his crate until you have had time to clean up his accident. Then release him to the family area and watch him more closely than before. Chances are, his accident was a result of your not picking up his signal or waiting too long before offering him the opportunity to relieve himself. Never hold a grudge against the puppy for accidents.

Let the puppy learn that going outdoors means it is time to relieve himself, not play. Once trained, he will be able to play indoors and out and still differentiate between the times for play versus the times for relief.

Help him develop regular hours for naps, being alone, playing by himself and just resting, all in his crate. Encourage him to entertain himself while you are busy with your activities. Let him learn that having you near is comforting, but it is not your main purpose in life to provide him with undivided attention.

Each time you put a puppy in his own area, use the same command, whatever suits best. Soon he will run to his crate or special area when he hears you say those words.

Crate training provides safety for you, the puppy and the home. It also provides the puppy with a feeling of security, and that helps the puppy achieve self-confidence and clean habits.

Remember that one of the primary ingredients in house-training your puppy is control. Regardless of your lifestyle, there will always be occasions when you will need to have a place where your dog can stay and be happy and safe. Crate training is the answer for now and in the future.

In conclusion, a few key elements are really all you need for a successful house-training method—consistency, frequency, praise, control and supervision. By following these procedures with a normal, healthy puppy,

*Adults require daily physical activity, including games of fetch, chase and obedience practice.*

## PLAN TO PLAY

The puppy should also have regular play and exercise sessions when he is with you or a family member. Exercise for a very young puppy can consist of a short walk around the house or garden. Playing can include fetching games with a large ball or a special raggy. (All puppies teethe and need soft things upon which to chew.) Remember to restrict play periods to indoors within his living area (the family room, for example) until he is completely house-trained.

you and the puppy will soon be past the stage of 'accidents' and ready to move on to a full and rewarding life together.

## ROLES OF DISCIPLINE, REWARD AND PUNISHMENT

Discipline, training one to act in accordance with rules, brings order to life. It is as simple as that. Without discipline, particularly in a group society, chaos reigns supreme and the group will eventually perish. Humans and canines are social animals and need some form of discipline in order to function effectively. They must procure food, protect their home base and their young and reproduce to keep the species going.

If there were no discipline in the lives of social animals, they would eventually die from starva-

tion and/or predation by other stronger animals.

In the case of domestic canines, dogs need discipline in their lives in order to understand how their pack (you and other family members) functions and how they must act in order to survive.

A large humane society in a highly populated area recently surveyed dog owners regarding their satisfaction with their relationships with their dogs. People who had trained their dogs were 75% more satisfied with their pets than those who had never trained their dogs.

Dr Edward Thorndike, a psychologist, established *Thorndike's Theory of Learning*, which states that a behaviour that results in a pleasant event tends to be repeated. A behaviour that results in an unpleasant event tends not to be repeated. It is this theory on which training methods are based today. For example, if you manipulate a dog to perform a specific behaviour and reward him for doing it, he is likely to do it again because he enjoyed the end result.

Occasionally, punishment, a penalty inflicted for an offence, is necessary. The best type of punishment often comes from an outside source. For example, a child is told not to touch the stove because he may get burned. He disobeys and touches the stove. In

## HOW TO WEAN THE 'TREAT HOG'

If you have trained your dog by rewarding him with a treat each time he performs a command, he may soon decide that without the treat, he won't sit, stay or come. The best way to fix this problem is to start asking your dog to do certain commands twice before being rewarded. Slowly increase the number of commands given and then vary the number: three sits and a treat one day, five sits for a biscuit the next day, etc. Your dog will soon realise that there is no set number of sits before he gets his reward, and he'll likely do it the first time you ask in the hope of being rewarded sooner rather than later.

doing so, he receives a burn. From that time on, he respects the heat of the stove and avoids contact with it. Therefore, a behaviour that results in an unpleasant event tends not to be repeated.

A good example of a dog learning the hard way is the dog who chases the house cat. He is told many times to leave the cat alone, yet he persists in teasing the cat. Then, one day he begins chasing the cat but the cat turns and swipes a claw across the dog's face, leaving him with a painful gash on his nose. The final result is that the dog stops chasing the cat.

## TRAINING EQUIPMENT

### COLLAR AND LEAD

For a Field Spaniel, the collar and lead that you use for training must be one with which you are easily able to work, not too heavy for the dog and perfectly safe.

### TREATS

Have a bag of treats on hand. Something nutritious and easy to swallow works best. Use a soft treat, a chunk of cheese or a piece of cooked chicken rather than a dry biscuit. By the time the dog has finished chewing a dry treat, he will forget why he is being rewarded in the first place! Using food rewards will not teach a dog to beg at the table—the only way to teach a dog to beg at the table is to give him food from the table. In

training, rewarding the dog with a food treat will help him associate praise and the treats with learning new behaviours that obviously please his owner.

## TRAINING BEGINS: ASK THE DOG A QUESTION

In order to teach your dog anything, you must first get his attention. After all, he cannot learn anything if he is looking away from you with his mind on something else.

To get his attention, ask him, 'School?' and immediately walk over to him and give him a treat as you tell him 'Good dog.' Wait a minute or two and repeat the routine, this time with a treat in your hand as you approach within a foot of the dog. Do not go directly to him, but stop about a foot short of him and hold out the treat as you ask, 'School?' He will see you approaching with a treat in your hand and most likely begin walking toward you. As you

### FEAR AGGRESSION

Pups who are subjected to physical abuse during training commonly end up with behavioural problems as adults. One common result of abuse is fear aggression, in which a dog will lash out, bare his teeth, snarl and finally bite someone by whom he feels threatened. For example, your daughter may be playing with the dog one afternoon. As they play hide-and-seek, she backs the dog into a corner and, as she attempts to tease him playfully, he bites her hand. Examine the cause of this behaviour. Did your daughter ever hit the dog? Did someone who resembles your daughter hit or scream at the dog?

Fortunately, fear aggression is relatively easy to correct. Have your daughter engage in only positive activities with the dog, such as feeding, petting and walking. She should not give any corrections or negative feedback. If the dog still growls or cowers away from her, allow someone else to accompany them. After approximately one week, the dog should feel that he can rely on her for many positive things, and he will also be prevented from reacting fearfully towards anyone who might resemble her.

### FAMILY TIES

If you have other pets in the home and/or interact often with the pets of friends and other family members, your pup will respond to those pets in much the same manner as you do. It is only when you show fear of or resentment toward another animal that he will act fearful or unfriendly.

meet, give him the treat and praise again.

The third time, ask the question, have a treat in your hand and walk only a short distance toward the dog so that he must walk almost all the way to you. As he reaches you, give him

Training your
Field Spaniel to
sit upon
command is an
easy exercise and,
once
accomplished,
will give you
confidence in
further training
possibilities.

the treat and praise again.

By this time, the dog will probably be getting the idea that if he pays attention to you, especially when you ask that question, it will pay off in treats and enjoyable activities for him. In other words, he learns that 'school' means doing great things with you that are fun and result in positive attention for him.

Remember that the dog does not understand your verbal language; he only recognises sounds. Your question translates to a series of sounds for him, and those sounds become the signal to go to you and pay attention; if he does, he will get to interact with you plus receive treats and praise.

## THE BASIC COMMANDS

### TEACHING SIT

Now that you have the dog's attention, attach his lead and hold it in your left hand and a food treat in your right. Place your food hand at the dog's nose and let him lick the treat but not take it from you. Say 'Sit' and slowly raise your food hand from in front of the dog's nose up over his head so that he is looking at the ceiling. As he bends his head upward, he will have to bend his knees to maintain his balance. As he bends his knees, he will assume a sit position. At that point, release the food treat and praise lavishly with comments such as 'Good dog! Good sit!,' etc. Remember to always praise enthusiastically, because dogs relish verbal praise from their owners and feel so proud of themselves whenever they accomplish a behaviour.

You will not use food forever in getting the dog to obey your commands. Food is only used to teach new behaviours, and once the dog knows what you want when you give a specific command, you will wean him off the food treats but still maintain the verbal praise. After all, you will always have your voice with you, and there will be many times when you have no food rewards but expect the dog to obey.

### TEACHING DOWN

Teaching the down exercise is easy when you understand how the dog perceives the down position, and it is very difficult when you do not. Dogs perceive the down position as a submissive one, therefore teaching the down exercise using a forceful method can sometimes make the dog develop such a fear of the down that he either runs away when you say 'Down' or he attempts to snap at the person who tries to force him down.

Have the dog sit close alongside your left leg, facing in the same direction as you are. Hold the lead in your left hand and a food treat in your right. Now place your left hand lightly on the top of the dog's shoulders where they meet above the spinal cord. Do not push down on the dog's shoulders; simply rest your left hand there so you can guide the dog to lie down close to your left leg rather than to swing away from your side when he drops.

Now place the food hand at the dog's nose, say 'Down' very softly (almost a whisper), and slowly lower the food hand to the dog's front feet. When the food hand reaches the floor, begin moving it forward along the floor in front of the dog. Keep talking softly to the dog, saying things like, 'Do you want this treat? You can do this, good dog.' Your reassuring tone of voice will help calm the dog as he tries to follow the food hand in order to get the treat.

When the dog's elbows touch the floor, release the food and praise softly. Try to get the dog to

maintain that down position for several seconds before you let him sit up again. The goal here is to get the dog to settle down and not feel threatened in the down position.

### TEACHING STAY

It is easy to teach the dog to stay in either a sit or a down position.

## DOUBLE JEOPARDY

A dog in jeopardy never lies down. He stays alert on his feet because instinct tells him that he may have to run away or fight for his survival. Therefore, if a dog feels threatened or anxious, he will not lie down. Consequently, it is important to have the dog calm and relaxed as he learns the down exercise.

## CONSISTENCY PAYS OFF

Dogs need consistency in their feeding schedule, exercise and toilet breaks, and in the verbal commands you use. If you use 'Stay' on Monday and 'Stay here, please' on Tuesday, you will confuse your dog. Don't demand perfect behaviour during training classes and then let him have the run of the house the rest of the day. Above all, lavish praise on your pet consistently every time he does something right. The more he feels he is pleasing you, the more willing he will be to learn.

Again, we use food and praise during the teaching process as we help the dog to understand exactly what it is that we are expecting him to do.

To teach the sit/stay, start with the dog sitting on your left side as before and hold the lead in your left hand. Have a food treat in your right hand and place your food hand at the dog's nose. Say 'Stay' and step out on your right foot to stand directly in front of the dog, toe to toe, as he licks and nibbles the treat. Be sure to keep his head facing upward to maintain the sit position. Count to five and then swing around to stand next to the dog again with him on your left. As soon as you get back to the original position, release the food and praise lavishly.

To teach the down/stay, do the down as previously described. As soon as the dog lies down, say 'Stay' and step out on your right foot just as you did in the sit/stay. Count to five and then return to stand beside the dog with him on your left side. Release the treat and praise as always.

Within a week or ten days, you can begin to add a bit of distance between you and your dog when you leave him. When you do, use your left hand open with the palm facing the dog as a stay signal, much the same as the hand signal a constable uses to stop traffic at an intersection. Hold the food treat in your right hand as before, but this time the food is not touching the dog's nose. He will watch the food hand and quickly learn that he is going

## 'WHERE ARE YOU?'

When calling the dog, do not say 'Come.' Say things like, 'Rover, where are you? See if you can find me! I have a biscuit for you!' Keep up a constant line of chatter with coaxing sounds and frequent questions such as, 'Where are you?' The dog will learn to follow the sound of your voice to locate you and receive his reward.

the tone of his voice when he calls his dog. Hearing that desperation in his owner's voice, the dog fears the results of going to him and therefore either disobeys outright or runs in the opposite direction. The secret, therefore, is to teach the dog a game and, when you want him to come to you, simply play the game. It is practically a no-fail solution!

To begin, have several members of your family take a few food treats and each go into a different room in the house. Take

to get that treat as soon as you return to his side.

When you can stand 1 metre away from your dog for 30 seconds, you can then begin building time and distance in both stays. Eventually, the dog can be expected to remain in the stay position for prolonged periods of time until you return to him or call him to you. Always praise lavishly when he stays.

### TEACHING COME

If you make teaching 'come' an exciting experience, you should never have a 'student' that does not love the game or that fails to come when called. The secret, it seems, is never to teach the word 'come.'

At times when an owner most wants his dog to come when called, the owner is likely to be upset or anxious and he allows these feelings to come through in

## RELIABLE RECALL

It is essential a puppy be taught a reliable recall command (come). Field Spaniels not taught at an early age that coming when called is essential may become runners. It is for the good of the dog that a reliable recall is essential; a dog that does not reliably come when called cannot be called out of danger.

### 'COME' . . . BACK

Never call your dog to come to you for a correction or scold him when he reaches you. That is the quickest way to turn a 'Come' command into 'Go away fast!' Dogs think only in the present tense, and your dog will connect the scolding with coming to you, not with the misbehaviour of a few moments earlier.

turns calling the dog, and each person should celebrate the dog's finding him with a treat and lots of happy praise. When a person calls the dog, he is actually inviting the dog to find him and get a treat as a reward for 'winning.'

A few turns of the 'Where are you?' game and the dog will understand that everyone is playing the game and that each person has a big celebration awaiting his success at locating them. Once he learns to love the game, simply calling out 'Where are you?' will bring him running from wherever he is when he hears that all-important question.

The come command is recognised as one of the most important things to teach a dog, but there are trainers who work with thousands of dogs and never teach the actual word 'Come.' Yet these dogs will race to respond to a person who uses the dog's name followed by 'Where are you?' For example, a woman has a 12-year-old companion dog who went blind, but who never fails to locate her owner when asked, 'Where are you?'

Children, in particular, love to play this game with their dogs. Children can hide in smaller places like a shower or bath, behind a bed or under a table. The dog needs to work a little bit harder to find these hiding places, but when he does he loves to celebrate with a treat and a tussle with a favourite youngster.

### TUG OF WALK?

If you begin teaching the heel by taking long walks and letting the dog pull you along, he misinterprets this action as an acceptable form of taking a walk. When you pull back on the lead to counteract his pulling, he reads that tug as a signal to pull even harder!

**TRAINING TIP**

If you are walking your dog and he suddenly stops and looks straight into your eyes, ignore him. Pull the leash and lead him into the direction you want to walk.

### TEACHING HEEL

Heeling means that the dog walks beside the owner without pulling. It takes time and patience on the owner's part to succeed at teaching the dog that he (the owner) will not proceed unless the dog is walking calmly beside him. Pulling out ahead on the lead is definitely not acceptable.

Begin by holding the lead in your left hand as the dog sits beside your left leg. Move the loop end of the lead to your right hand but keep your left hand short on the lead so it keeps the dog in close next to you.

Say 'Heel' and step forward on your left foot. Keep the dog close to you and take three steps. Stop and have the dog sit next to you in what we now call the 'heel position.' Praise verbally, but do not touch the dog. Hesitate a moment and begin again with 'Heel,' taking three steps and stopping, at which point the dog is told to sit again.

Your goal here is to have the dog walk those three steps without pulling on the lead. Once he will walk calmly beside you

**FETCH!**

Play fetch games with your puppy in an enclosed or secluded area where he can retrieve his toy and bring it back to you. Always use a toy or object designated just for this purpose. Never use a shoe, stocking or other item he may later confuse with those in your wardrobe or underneath your chair.

for three steps without pulling, increase the number of steps you take to five. When he will walk politely beside you while you take five steps, you can increase the length of your walk to ten steps. Keep increasing the length of your stroll until the dog will walk quietly beside you without pulling

If you have any intention of showing your Field Spaniel, commit to training from the beginning. You should train your dog to stay and stand at home before attending a show.

## HEELING WELL

Teach your dog to HEEL in an enclosed area. Once you think the dog will obey reliably and you want to attempt advanced obedience exercises such as off-lead heeling, test him in a fenced-in area so he cannot run away.

as long as you want him to heel. When you stop heeling, indicate to the dog that the exercise is over by verbally praising as you pet him and say 'OK, good dog.' The 'OK' is used as a release word, meaning that the exercise is finished and the dog is free to relax.

If you are dealing with a dog who insists on pulling you around, simply 'put on your brakes' and stand your ground until the dog realises that the two of you are not going anywhere until he is beside you and moving at your pace, not his. It may take some time just standing there to convince the dog that you are the leader and you will be the one to decide on the direction and speed of your travel.

Each time the dog looks up at you or slows down to give a slack lead between the two of you, quietly praise him and say, 'Good heel. Good dog.' Eventually, the dog will begin to respond and within a few days he will be walking politely beside you without pulling on the lead. At

first, the training sessions should be kept short and very positive; soon the dog will be able to walk nicely with you for increasingly longer distances. Remember also to give the dog free time and the opportunity to run and play when you have finished heel practice.

## HELPING PAWS

Your dog may not be the next Lassie, but every pet has the potential to do some tricks well. Identify his natural talents and hone them. Is your dog always happy and upbeat? Teach him to wag his tail or give you his paw on command. Real homebodies can be trained to do household chores, such as carrying dirty washing or retrieving the morning paper.

## WEANING OFF FOOD IN TRAINING

Food is used in training new behaviours. Once the dog understands what behaviour goes with a specific command, it is time to start weaning him off the food treats. At first, give a treat after each exercise. Then, start to give a treat only after every other exercise. Mix up the times when you offer a food reward and the times when you only offer praise so that the dog will never know when he is going to receive both food and praise and when he is going to receive only praise. This is called a variable ratio reward system and it proves successful because there is always the chance that the owner will produce a treat, so the dog never stops trying for that reward. No matter what, ALWAYS give verbal praise.

## OBEDIENCE CLASSES

It is a good idea to enrol in an obedience class if one is available in your area. If yours is a show dog, ringcraft classes would be more appropriate. Many areas have dog clubs that offer basic obedience training as well as preparatory classes for obedience competition. There are also local dog trainers who offer similar classes.

At dog shows and trials, dogs can earn titles at various levels of competition. The beginning levels of competition include basic behaviours such as sit, down, heel, etc. The more advanced levels of competition include jumping, retrieving, scent discrimination and signal work. The advanced levels require a dog and owner to put a lot of time and effort into their training, and the titles that can be earned at these levels of competition are very prestigious.

## OTHER ACTIVITIES FOR LIFE

Whether a dog is trained in the structured environment of a class or alone with his owner at home, there are many activities that can bring fun and rewards to both owner and dog once they have mastered basic control.

Teaching the dog to help out around the home, in the garden or on the farm provides great satisfaction to both dog and owner. In addition, the dog's help makes life a little easier for his owner and raises his stature as a valued companion to his family. It helps give the dog a purpose by occupying his mind and providing an outlet for his energy.

If you are interested in participating in organised competition with your Field Spaniel, there is a variety of activities in which you and your dog can become involved.

### HUNTING

As a member of the Gundog group, Field Spaniels are well suited for hunting game as appropriate to their size. They are often used to locate and flush upland game birds,

## ASSISTANCE AND THERAPY WORK

A number of Field Spaniels actively participate as therapy dogs, ranging from specially trained dogs who visit nursing homes and other group-care facilities to dogs who actively provide assistance. In functioning as an assistance dog, regard must be given to the overall size of the Field Spaniel. For example, a Field Spaniel is not going to make a suitable guide dog for the blind due to its more compact size but does well as a hearing dog. Their natural affinity for humans, desire to please and problem-solving ability make them well suited to this sort of training.

## AGILITY AND OBEDIENCE

A trained Field Spaniel is a joy to live with as training and activity provide an appropriate outlet for their considerable ability to learn and solve problems. Field Spaniels enjoy participating in activities with their owners and agility and obedience are two types of competition in which both dog and handler play active roles. Agility and advanced obedience competitions often require jumping. Care must be taken to avoid stress on developing skeletal structures. Jumping must be taught systematically and with care to assure good form and prevent avoidable injury. Begin with very low jump heights and progress to greater heights slowly. The Kennel Club requires that dogs be at least 12 to 18 months of age before agility training begins.

---

**DID YOU KNOW?**

Occasionally, a dog and owner who have not attended formal classes have been able to earn entry-level titles by obtaining competition rules and regulations from a local kennel club and practising on their own to a degree of perfection. Obtaining the higher level titles, however, almost always requires extensive training under the tutelage of experienced instructors. In addition, the more difficult levels require more specialised equipment whereas the lower levels do not.

---

later retrieving the shot game to the handler back from land or water. Fanciers have also reported success in using the Field Spaniel on rabbit. They are typically tenacious and thorough in working cover.

## TRACKING

Field Spaniels excel in tracking. The large nose of the Field Spaniel is ideally suited and able to work in a variety of situations that capitalise on their purposeful and powerful scenting ability. Field Spaniels have been trained to use their noses in search and rescue work, narcotics detection and other similar endeavours in addition to training for participation in standardised tracking tests offered by some kennel associations.

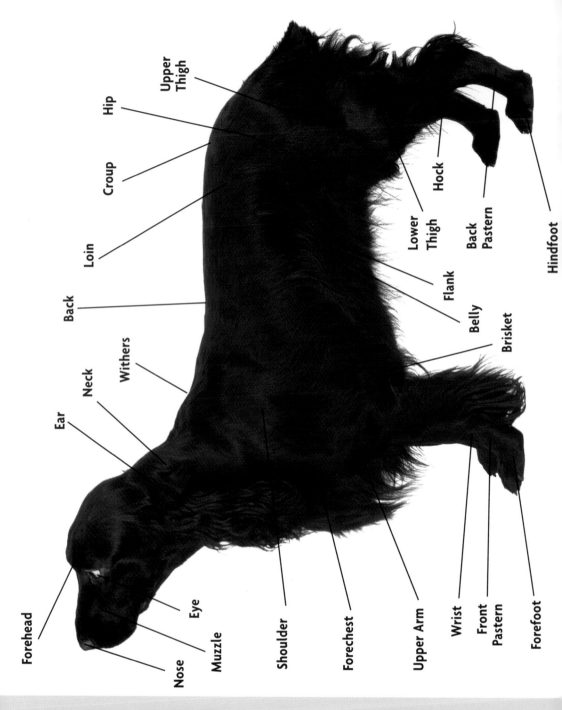

Upper Thigh

Hip

Croup

Loin

Back

Withers

Neck

Ear

Forehead

Hock

Lower Thigh

Back Pastern

Hindfoot

Flank

Belly

Brisket

Eye

Muzzle

Nose

Shoulder

Forechest

Upper Arm

Wrist

Front Pastern

Forefoot

# PHYSICAL STRUCTURE OF THE FIELD SPANIEL

Dogs suffer from many of the same physical illnesses as people. They might even share many of the same psychological problems. Since people usually know more about human diseases than canine maladies, many of the terms used in this chapter will be familiar but not necessarily those used by veterinary surgeons. We will use the term *x-ray*, instead of the more acceptable term *radiograph*. We will also use the familiar term *symptoms* even though dogs don't have symptoms, which are verbal descriptions of the patient's feelings; dogs have *clinical signs*. Since dogs can't speak, we have to look for clinical signs...but we still use the term *symptoms* in this book.

As a general rule, medicine is *practised*. That term is not arbitrary. Medicine is a constantly changing art as we learn more and more about genetics, electronic aids (like CAT scans) and daily laboratory advances. There are many dog maladies, like canine hip dysplasia, which are not universally treated in the same manner. Some veterinary surgeons opt for surgery more often than others do.

## SELECTING A VETERINARY SURGEON

Your selection of a veterinary surgeon should not be based upon personality (as most are) but upon their convenience to your home. You want a vet who is close because you might have emergencies or need to make multiple visits for treatments. You want a vet who has services that you might require such as tattooing and grooming, as well as sophisticated pet supplies and a good reputation for ability and responsiveness. There is nothing more frustrating than having to wait a day or more to get a response from your veterinary surgeon.

All veterinary surgeons are licensed and their diplomas and/or certificates should be displayed in their waiting rooms. There are, however, many veterinary specialities that usually require further studies and internships. There are specialists in heart problems (veterinary cardiologists), skin problems (veterinary dermatologists), teeth and gum problems (veterinary dentists), eye problems (veterinary ophthalmologists) and x-rays (veterinary radiologists), as well

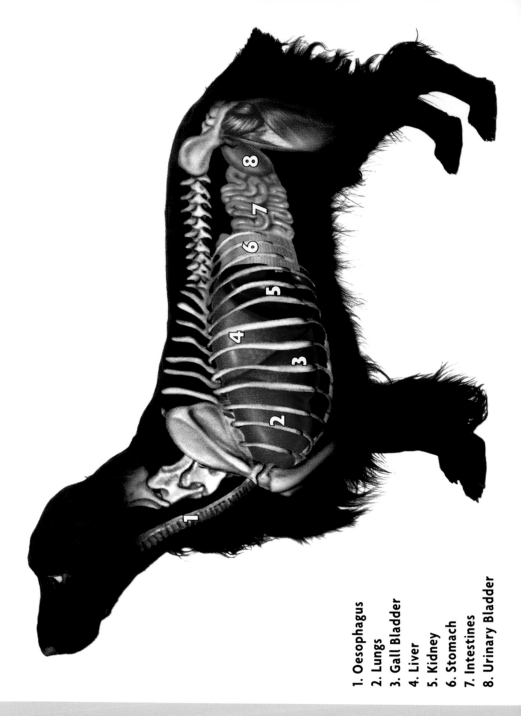

1. Oesophagus
2. Lungs
3. Gall Bladder
4. Liver
5. Kidney
6. Stomach
7. Intestines
8. Urinary Bladder

# INTERNAL ORGANS OF THE FIELD SPANIEL

as vets who have specialities in bones, muscles or other organs. Most veterinary surgeons do routine surgery such as neutering, stitching up wounds and docking tails for those breeds in which such is required for show purposes. When the problem affecting your dog is serious, it is not unusual or impudent to get another medical opinion, although in Britain you are obliged to advise the vets concerned about this. You might also want to compare costs among several veterinary surgeons. Sophisticated health care and veterinary services can be very costly. It is not infrequent that important decisions are based upon financial considerations.

## PREVENTATIVE MEDICINE

It is much easier, less costly and more effective to practise preventative medicine than to fight bouts of illness and disease. Properly bred puppies come from parents who were selected based upon their genetic disease profile. Their

**Breakdown of Veterinary Income by Category**

| | |
|---|---|
| 2% | Dentistry |
| 4% | Radiology |
| 12% | Surgery |
| 15% | Vaccinations |
| 19% | Laboratory |
| 23% | Examinations |
| 25% | Medicines |

mothers should have been vaccinated, free of all internal and external parasites and properly nourished. For these reasons, a visit to the veterinary surgeon who cared for the dam is recommended. The dam can pass on disease resistance to her puppies, which can last for eight to ten weeks. She can also pass on parasites and many infections. That's why you should visit the veterinary surgeon who cared for the dam.

### VACCINATION SCHEDULING

Most vaccinations are given by injection and should only be done by a veterinary surgeon. Both he and you should keep a record of the date of the injection, the identification of the vaccine and the amount given. Some vets give a first vaccination at eight weeks, but most dog breeders prefer the course not to commence until about ten weeks because of

**DID YOU KNOW?**
Male dogs are neutered. The operation removes the testicles and requires that the dog be anaesthetised. Recovery takes about one week. Females are spayed. This is major surgery and it usually takes a bitch two weeks to recover.

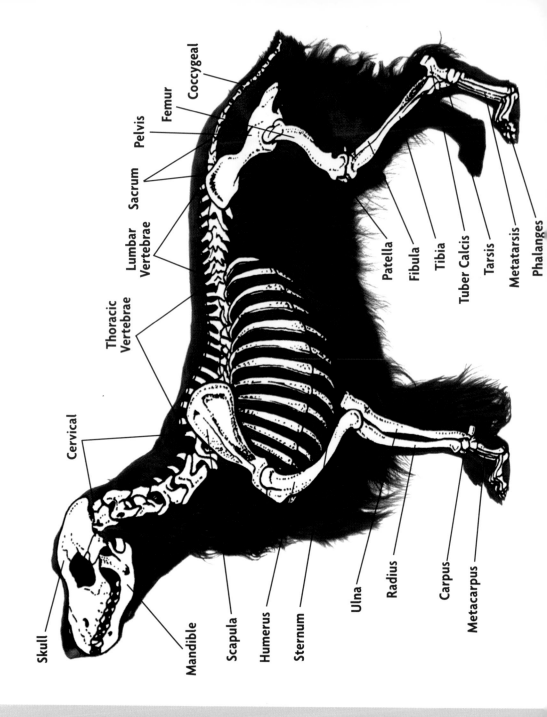

Coccygeal
Femur
Pelvis
Sacrum
Lumbar Vertebrae
Thoracic Vertebrae
Cervical
Skull
Mandible
Scapula
Humerus
Sternum
Ulna
Radius
Carpus
Metacarpus
Patella
Fibula
Tibia
Tuber Calcis
Tarsis
Metatarsis
Phalanges

# SKELETAL STRUCTURE OF THE FIELD SPANIEL

negating any antibodies passed on by the dam. The vaccination scheduling is usually based on a 15-day cycle. You must take your vet's advice regarding when to vaccinate as this may differ according to the vaccine used. Most vaccinations immunize your puppy against viruses.

The usual vaccines contain immunizing doses of several different viruses such as distemper, parvovirus, parain-

### BE CAREFUL WHERE YOU WALK YOUR DOG
Dogs who have been exposed to lawns sprayed with herbicides have double and triple the rate of malignant lymphoma. Town dogs are especially at risk, as they are exposed to tailored lawns and gardens. Dogs perspire and absorb through their footpads. Be careful where your dog walks and always avoid any area that appears yellowed from chemical overspray.

### PROPER DIET
Feeding your dog properly is very important. An incorrect diet could affect the dog's health, behaviour and nervous system, possibly making a normal dog into an aggressive one.

fluenza and hepatitis, although some veterinary surgeons recommend separate vaccines for each disease. There are other vaccines available when the puppy is at risk. You should rely upon professional advice. This is especially true for the booster-shot programme. Most vaccination programmes require a booster when the puppy is a year old and once a year thereafter. In some cases, circumstances may require more or less frequent immunizations. Kennel cough, more

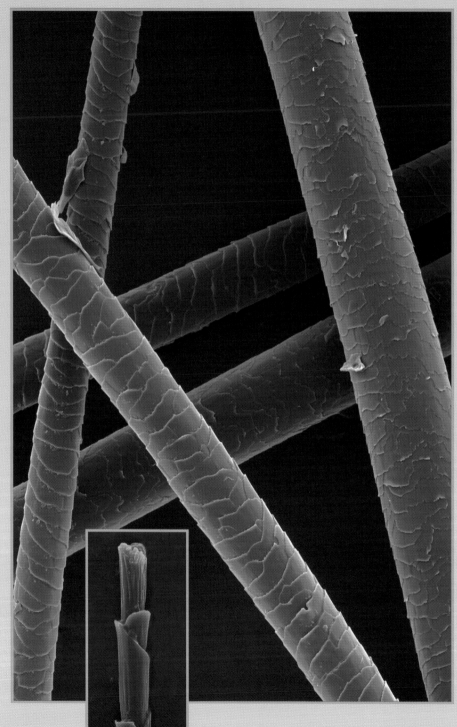

Normal hairs of a dog enlarged 200 times original size. The cuticle (outer covering) is clean and healthy. Unlike human hair that grows from the base, a dog's hair also grows from the end, as shown in the inset. Scanning electron micrographs by Dr Dennis Kunkel, University of Hawaii.

S.E.M. BY DR DENNIS KUNKEL, UNIVERSITY OF HAWAII

# HEALTH AND VACCINATION SCHEDULE

| Age in Weeks: | 6th | 8th | 10th | 12th | 14th | 16th | 20-24th | 1 yr |
|---|---|---|---|---|---|---|---|---|
| Worm Control | ✔ | ✔ | ✔ | ✔ | ✔ | ✔ | ✔ | |
| Neutering | | | | | | | | ✔ |
| Heartworm | | ✔ | | ✔ | | ✔ | ✔ | |
| Parvovirus | ✔ | | ✔ | | ✔ | | ✔ | ✔ |
| Distemper | | ✔ | | ✔ | | ✔ | | ✔ |
| Hepatitis | | ✔ | | ✔ | | ✔ | | ✔ |
| Leptospirosis | | | | | | | | ✔ |
| Parainfluenza | ✔ | | ✔ | | ✔ | | | ✔ |
| Dental Examination | | ✔ | | | | | ✔ | ✔ |
| Complete Physical | | ✔ | | | | | ✔ | ✔ |
| Coronavirus | | | | ✔ | | | ✔ | ✔ |
| Kennel Cough | ✔ | | | | | | | |
| Hip Dysplasia | | | | | | | | ✔ |
| Rabies | | | | | | | ✔ | |

Vaccinations are not instantly effective. It takes about two weeks for the dog's immune system to develop antibodies. Most vaccinations require annual booster shots. Your veterinary surgeon should guide you in this regard.

formally known as tracheobronchitis, is treated with a vaccine that is sprayed into the dog's nostrils. Kennel cough is usually included in routine vaccination, but this is often not so effective as for other major diseases.

**WEANING TO FIVE MONTHS OLD**
Puppies should be weaned by the time they are about two months old. A puppy that remains for at least eight weeks with its mother and littermates usually adapts better to other dogs and people later in its life.

Some new owners have their puppy examined by a veterinary surgeon immediately, which is a good idea. Vaccination programmes usually begin when the puppy is very young.

## PUPPY VACCINATIONS
Your veterinary surgeon will probably recommend that your puppy be vaccinated before you take him outside. There are airborne diseases, parasite eggs in the grass and unexpected visits from other dogs that might be dangerous to your puppy's health.

The puppy will have its teeth examined and have its skeletal conformation and general health checked prior to certification by the veterinary surgeon. Puppies in certain breeds have problems with their kneecaps, cataracts and other eye problems, heart murmurs and undescended testicles. They may also have personality problems and your veterinary surgeon might have training in temperament evaluation.

### FIVE TO TWELVE MONTHS OF AGE

Unless you intend to breed or show your dog, neutering the puppy at six months of age is recommended. Discuss this with your veterinary surgeon. Neutering has proven to be extremely beneficial to both male and female puppies. Besides eliminating the possibility of pregnancy, it inhibits (but does not prevent) breast cancer in bitches and prostate cancer in male dogs. Under no circum-

### KNOW WHEN TO POSTPONE A VACCINATION

While the visit to the vet is costly, it is never advisable to update a vaccination when visiting with a sick or pregnant dog. Vaccinations should be avoided for all elderly dogs. If your dog is showing the signs of any illness or any medical condition, no matter how serious or mild, including skin irritations, do not vaccinate. Likewise, a lame dog should never be vaccinated; any dog undergoing surgery or on any immunosuppressant drugs should not be vaccinated until fully recovered.

stances should a bitch be spayed prior to her first season.

Your veterinary surgeon should provide your puppy with a thorough dental evaluation at six months of age, ascertaining whether all the permanent teeth have erupted properly. A home dental care regimen should be initiated at six months, including brushing weekly and providing good dental devices (such as nylon bones). Regular dental care promotes healthy teeth, fresh breath and a longer life.

### ONE TO SEVEN YEARS

Once a year, your grown dog should visit the vet for an examination and vaccination

### VACCINE ALLERGIES

Vaccines do not work all the time. Sometimes dogs are allergic to them and many times the antibodies, which are supposed to be stimulated by the vaccine, just are not produced. You should keep your dog in the veterinary clinic for an hour after it is vaccinated to be sure there are no allergic reactions.

boosters, if needed. Some vets recommend blood tests, thyroid level check and dental evaluation to accompany these annual visits. A thorough clinical evaluation by the vet can provide critical background information for your dog. Blood tests are often performed at one year of age, and dental examinations around the third or fourth birthday. In the long run, quality preventative care for your pet can save money, teeth and lives.

## MORE THAN VACCINES

Vaccinations help prevent your new puppy from contracting diseases, but they do not cure them. Proper nutrition as well as parasite control keep your dog healthy and less susceptible to many dangerous diseases. Remember that your dog depends on you to ensure his well-being.

# DISEASE REFERENCE CHART

| | What is it? | What causes it? | Symptoms |
|---|---|---|---|
| **Leptospirosis** | Severe disease that affects the internal organs; can be spread to people. | A bacterium, which is often carried by rodents, that enters through mucous membranes and spreads quickly throughout the body. | Range from fever, vomiting and loss of appetite in less severe cases to shock, irreversible kidney damage and possibly death in most severe cases. |
| **Rabies** | Potentially deadly virus that infects warm-blooded mammals. Not seen in United Kingdom. | Bite from a carrier of the virus, mainly wild animals. | 1st stage: dog exhibits change in behaviour, fear. 2nd stage: dog's behaviour becomes more aggressive. 3rd stage: loss of coordination, trouble with bodily functions. |
| **Parvovirus** | Highly contagious virus, potentially deadly. | Ingestion of the virus, which is usually spread through the faeces of infected dogs. | Most common: severe diarrhoea. Also vomiting, fatigue, lack of appetite. |
| **Kennel cough** | Contagious respiratory infection. | Combination of types of bacteria and virus. Most common: *Bordetella bronchiseptica* bacteria and parainfluenza virus. | Chronic cough. |
| **Distemper** | Disease primarily affecting respiratory and nervous system. | Virus that is related to the human measles virus. | Mild symptoms such as fever, lack of appetite and mucous secretion progress to evidence of brain damage, 'hard pad.' |
| **Hepatitis** | Virus primarily affecting the liver. | Canine adenovirus type I (CAV-1). Enters system when dog breathes in particles. | Lesser symptoms include listlessness, diarrhoea, vomiting. More severe symptoms include 'blue-eye' (clumps of virus in eye). |
| **Coronavirus** | Virus resulting in digestive problems. | Virus is spread through infected dog's faeces. | Stomach upset evidenced by lack of appetite, vomiting, diarrhoea. |

## DENTAL HEALTH

A dental examination is in order when the dog is between six months and one year of age so any permanent teeth that have erupted incorrectly can be corrected. It is important to begin a brushing routine, preferably using a two-sided brushing technique, whereby both sides of the tooth are brushed at the same time. Durable nylon and safe edible chews should be a part of your puppy's arsenal for good health, good teeth and pleasant breath. The vast majority of dogs three to four years old and older has diseases of the gums from lack of dental attention. Using the various types of dental chews can be very effective in controlling dental plaque.

## SKIN PROBLEMS IN FIELD SPANIELS

Veterinary surgeons are consulted by dog owners for skin problems more than any other group of diseases or maladies. Dogs' skin is almost as sensitive as human skin and both suffer almost the same ailments (though the occurrence of acne in dogs is rare!). For this reason, veterinary dermatology has developed into a speciality practised by many veterinary surgeons.

Since many skin problems have visual symptoms that are almost identical, it requires the skill of an experienced veterinary dermatologist to identify and cure many of the more severe skin disorders. Pet shops sell many treatments for skin problems but most of the treatments are directed at symptoms and not the underlying problem(s). If your dog is suffering from a skin disorder, you should seek professional assistance as quickly as possible. As with all diseases, the earlier a problem is identified and treated, the more successful is the cure.

### HEREDITARY SKIN DISORDERS

Veterinary dermatologists are currently researching a number of skin disorders that are believed to have an hereditary basis. These inherited diseases are transmitted by both parents, who appear (phenotypically) normal but have a recessive gene for the disease,

## The Eyes Have It!

Eye disease is more prevalent among dogs than most people think, ranging from slight infections that are easily treated to serious complications that can lead to permanent sight loss. Eye diseases need veterinary attention in their early stages to prevent irreparable damage. This list provides descriptions of some common eye diseases:

**Cataracts**: Symptoms are white or grey discoloration of the eye lens and pupil, which causes fuzzy or completely obscured vision. Surgical treatment is required to remove the damaged lens and replace it with an artificial one.

**Conjunctivitis:** An inflammation of the mucous membrane that lines the eye socket, leaving the eyes red and puffy with excessive discharge. This condition is easily treated with antibiotics.

**Corneal damage:** The cornea is the transparent covering of the iris and pupil. Injuries are difficult to detect, but manifest themselves in surface abnormality, redness, pain and discharge. Most infections of the cornea are treated with antibiotics and require immediate medical attention.

**Dry eye:** This condition is caused by deficient production of tears that lubricate and protect the eye surface. A telltale sign is yellow-green discharge. Left undiagnosed, your dog will experience considerable pain, infections and possibly blindness. Dry eye is commonly treated with antibiotics, although more advanced cases may require surgery.

**Glaucoma:** This is caused by excessive fluid pressure in the eye. Symptoms are red eyes, grey or blue discoloration, pain, enlarged eyeballs and loss of vision. Antibiotics sometimes help, but surgery may be needed.

meaning that they carry, but are not affected by, the disease. These diseases pose serious problems to breeders because in some instances there is no method of identifying carriers. Often the secondary diseases associated with these skin conditions are even more debilitating than the disorder itself, including cancers and respiratory problems; others can be lethal.

Among the hereditary skin disorders, for which the mode of inheritance is known, are: acrodermatitis, cutaneous asthenia (Ehlers-Danlos syndrome), sebaceous adenitis, cyclic hematopoiesis, dermatomyositis, IgA deficiency, colour dilution alopaecia and nodular dermatofibrosis. Some of these disorders are limited to one or two breeds and others affect a large number of breeds. All inherited diseases must be diagnosed and treated by a veterinary specialist.

### PARASITE BITES

Many of us are allergic to insect bites. The bites itch, erupt and may even become infected. Dogs have the same reaction to fleas, ticks and/or mites. When an insect lands on you, you have the chance to whisk it away with your hand. Unfortunately, when your dog is bitten by a flea, tick or mite, it can only scratch it away or bite it. By the time the dog has been bitten, the parasite has done some of its damage. It may also have laid eggs to cause further problems in the near future. The itching from parasite bites is probably due to the saliva injected into the site when the parasite sucks the dog's blood.

### AUTO-IMMUNE SKIN CONDITIONS

Auto-immune skin conditions are commonly referred to as being allergic to yourself, while allergies are usually inflammatory reactions to an outside stimulus. Auto-immune diseases cause serious damage to the tissues that are involved.

The best known auto-immune disease is lupus, which affects people as well as dogs. The

symptoms are variable and may affect the kidneys, bones, blood chemistry and skin. It can be fatal to both dogs and humans, though it is not thought to be transmissible. It is usually successfully treated with cortisone, prednisone or a similar corticosteroid, but extensive use of these drugs can have harmful side effects.

### AIRBORNE ALLERGIES

An interesting allergy is pollen allergy. Humans have hay fever, rose fever and other fevers with which they suffer during the pollinating season. Many dogs suffer the same allergies. When the pollen count is high, your dog

not eliminate the problem if the element to which the dog is allergic is contained in the new brand.

Recognising a food allergy is difficult. Humans vomit or have rashes when they eat a food to which they are allergic. Dogs neither vomit nor (usually) develop a rash. They react in the same manner as they do to an airborne or flea allergy; they itch, scratch and bite, thus making the diagnosis extremely difficult.

Dogs, like humans and other animals, can be allergic to airborne substances like pollen, mould spores or fertilisers and pesticides that might be carried his way by the wind.

might suffer but don't expect him to sneeze and have a runny nose like humans. Dogs react to pollen allergies the same way they react to fleas—they scratch and bite themselves.

Dogs, like humans, can be tested for allergens. Discuss the testing with your veterinary dermatologist.

## FOOD PROBLEMS

### FOOD ALLERGIES

Dogs are allergic to many foods that are best-sellers and highly recommended by breeders and veterinary surgeons. Changing the brand of food that you buy may

## PET ADVANTAGES

If you do not intend to show or breed your new puppy, your veterinary surgeon will probably recommend that you spay your female or neuter your male. Some people believe neutering leads to weight gain, but if you feed and exercise your dog properly, this is easily avoided. Spaying or neutering can actually have many positive outcomes, such as:

• training becomes easier, as the dog focuses less on the urge to mate and more on you!

• females are protected from unplanned pregnancy as well as ovarian and uterine cancers.

• males are guarded from testicular tumours and have a reduced risk of developing prostate cancer.

Talk to your vet regarding the right age to spay/neuter and other aspects of the procedure.

### PARVO FOR THE COURSE

Canine parvovirus is a highly contagious disease that attacks puppies and older dogs. Spread through contact with infected faeces, parvovirus causes bloody diarrhoea, vomiting, heart damage, dehydration, shock and death. To prevent this tragedy, have your puppy begin his series of vaccinations at six to eight weeks of age. Be aware that the virus is easily spread and is carried on a dog's hair, feet, water bowls and other objects, as well as on people's shoes and clothing.

While pollen allergies and parasite bites are usually seasonal, food allergies are year-round problems.

### FOOD INTOLERANCE

Food intolerance is the inability of the dog to completely digest certain foods. Puppies that may have done very well on their mother's milk may not do well on cow's milk. The result of this food intolerance may be loose bowels, passing gas and stomach pains. These are the only obvious symptoms of food intolerance and that makes diagnosis difficult.

## Vitamins Recommended for Dogs

Some breeders and vets recommend the supplementation of vitamins to a dog's diet—others do not. Before embarking on a vitamin programme, consult your vet.

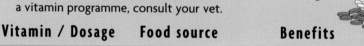

| Vitamin / Dosage | Food source | Benefits |
| --- | --- | --- |
| A / 10,000 IU/week | Eggs, butter, yoghurt, meat | Skin, eyes, hind legs, haircoat |
| B / Varies | Organs, cottage cheese, sardines | Appetite, fleas, heart, skin and coat |
| C / 2000 mg+ | Fruit, legumes, leafy green vegetables | Healing, arthritis, kidneys |
| D / Varies | Cod liver, cheese, organs, eggs | Bones, teeth, endocrine system |
| E / 250 IU daily | Leafy green vegetables, meat, wheat germ oil | Skin, muscles, nerves, healing, digestion |
| F / Varies | Fish oils, raw meat | Heart, skin, coat, fleas |
| K / Varies | Naturally in body, not through food | Blood clotting |

### TREATING FOOD PROBLEMS

It is possible to handle food allergies and food intolerance yourself. Put your dog on a diet that it has never had. Obviously if it has never eaten this new food, it can't have been allergic or intolerant of it. Start with a single ingredient that is not in the dog's diet at the present time. Ingredients like chopped beef or fish are common in dogs' diets, so try something more exotic like rabbit, pheasant or even just vegetables. Keep the dog on this diet (with no additives) for a month. If the symptoms of food allergy or intolerance disappear, chances are your dog has a food allergy.

Don't think that the single ingredient cured the problem. You still must find a suitable diet and ascertain which ingredient in the

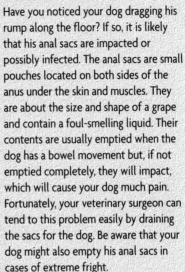

**A SKUNKY PROBLEM**
Have you noticed your dog dragging his rump along the floor? If so, it is likely that his anal sacs are impacted or possibly infected. The anal sacs are small pouches located on both sides of the anus under the skin and muscles. They are about the size and shape of a grape and contain a foul-smelling liquid. Their contents are usually emptied when the dog has a bowel movement but, if not emptied completely, they will impact, which will cause your dog much pain. Fortunately, your veterinary surgeon can tend to this problem easily by draining the sacs for the dog. Be aware that your dog might also empty his anal sacs in cases of extreme fright.

old diet was objectionable. This is most easily done by adding ingredients to the new diet one at a time. Let the dog stay on the modified diet for a month before you add another ingredient. Eventually, you will determine the ingredient that caused the adverse reaction.

An alternative method is to carefully study the ingredients in the diet to which your dog is allergic or intolerant. Identify the main ingredient in this diet and eliminate the main ingredient by buying a different food that does not have that ingredient. Keep experimenting until the symptoms disappear after one month on the new diet.

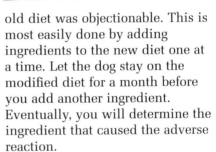

**VITAL SIGNS**
A dog's normal temperature is 101.5 degrees Fahrenheit. A range of between 100.0 and 102.5 degrees should be considered normal, as each dog's body sets its own temperature. It will be helpful if you take your dog's temperature when you know he is healthy and record it. Then, when you suspect that he is not feeling well, you will have a normal figure to compare the abnormal temperature against.

The normal pulse rate for a dog is between 100 and 125 beats per minute.

## EXTERNAL PARASITES

### FLEAS

Of all the problems to which dogs are prone, none is more well known and frustrating than fleas. Flea infestation is relatively simple to cure but difficult to prevent. Parasites that are harboured inside the body are a bit more difficult to eradicate but they are easier to control.

To control flea infestation, you have to understand the flea's life cycle. Fleas are often thought of as a summertime problem, but centrally heated homes have changed the patterns and fleas can be found at any time of the year. The most effective method of flea control is a two-stage approach: one stage to kill the adult fleas, and the other to control the development of pre-adult fleas. Unfortunately, no single active ingredient is effective against all stages of the life cycle.

### LIFE CYCLE STAGES

During its life, a flea will pass through four life stages: egg, larva, pupa and adult. The adult stage is the most visible and irritating stage of the flea life cycle, and this is

A scanning electron micrograph (S. E. M.) of a dog flea, *Ctenocephalides canis*.

S. E. M. BY DR DENNIS KUNKEL, UNIVERSITY OF HAWAII

Magnified head of a dog flea, *Ctenocephalides canis*.

S. E. M. BY DR DENNIS KUNKEL, UNIVERSITY OF HAWAII

## A Look at Fleas

Fleas have been around for millions of years and have adapted to changing host animals. They are able to go through a complete life cycle in less than one month or they can extend their lives to almost two years by remaining as pupae or cocoons. They do not need blood or any other food for up to 20 months.

They have been measured as being able to jump 300,000 times and can jump 150 times their length in any direction including straight up. Those are just a few of the reasons why they are so successful in infesting a dog!

why the majority of flea-control products concentrate on this stage. The fact is that adult fleas account for only 1% of the total flea population, and the other 99% exist in pre-adult stages, i.e. eggs, larvae and pupae. The pre-adult stages are barely visible to the naked eye.

### THE LIFE CYCLE OF THE FLEA

Eggs are laid on the dog, usually in quantities of about 20 or 30, several times a day. The female adult flea must have a blood meal before each egg-laying session. When first laid, the eggs will cling to the dog's fur, as the eggs are still moist.

However, they will quickly dry out and fall from the dog, especially if the dog moves around or scratches. Many eggs will fall off in the dog's favourite area or an area in which he spends a lot of time, such as his bed.

Once the eggs fall from the dog onto the carpet or furniture, they will hatch into larvae. This takes from one to ten days. Larvae are not particularly mobile, and will usually travel only a few inches from where they hatch. However, they do have a tendency to move away from light and heavy traffic— under furniture and behind doors

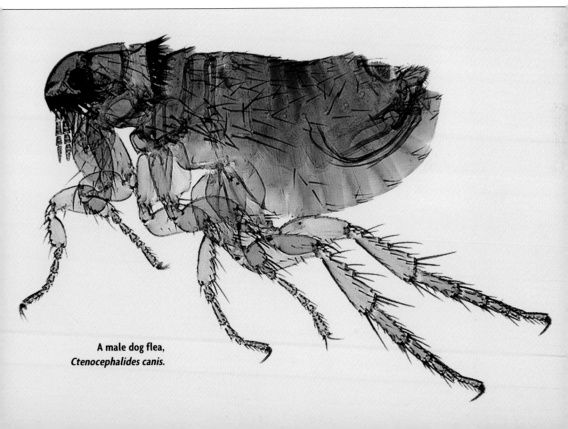

**A male dog flea,**
***Ctenocephalides canis.***

are common places to find high quantities of flea larvae.

The flea larvae feed on dead organic matter, including adult flea faeces, until they are ready to change into adult fleas. Fleas will usually remain as larvae for around seven days. After this period, the larvae will pupate into protective pupae. While inside the pupae, the larvae will undergo metamorphosis and change into adult fleas. This can take as little time as a few days, but the adult fleas can remain inside the pupae waiting to hatch for up to two years. The pupae are signalled to hatch by certain stimuli, such as physical pressure— the pupae's being stepped on, heat from an animal lying on the pupae or increased carbon dioxide levels and vibrations—indicating that a suitable host is available.

Once hatched, the adult flea must feed within a few days. Once the adult flea finds a host, it will not leave voluntarily. It only becomes dislodged by grooming or the host animal's scratching. The adult flea will remain on the host for the duration of its life unless forcibly removed.

**DID YOU KNOW?**
Never mix flea control products without first consulting your veterinary surgeon. Some products can become toxic when combined with others and can cause serious or fatal consequences.

**DID YOU KNOW?**
Flea-killers are poisonous. You should not spray these toxic chemicals on areas of a dog's body that he licks, on his genitals or on his face. Flea killers taken internally are a better answer, but check with your vet in case internal therapy is not advised for your dog.

### TREATING THE ENVIRONMENT AND THE DOG

Treating fleas should be a two-pronged attack. First, the environment needs to be treated; this includes carpets and furniture, especially the dog's bedding and areas underneath furniture. The environment should be treated with a household spray containing an Insect Growth Regulator (IGR) and an insecticide to kill the adult fleas. Most IGRs are effective against eggs and larvae; they actually mimic the fleas' own hormones and stop the eggs and larvae from developing into adult fleas. There are currently no treatments available to attack the pupa stage of the life cycle, so the adult insecticide is used to kill the newly hatched adult fleas before they find a host. Most IGRs are active for many months, whilst adult insecticides are only active for a few days.

Opposite page: A scanning electron micrograph of a dog or cat flea, *Ctenocephalides*, magnified more than 100x. This image has been colorized for effect.

# The Life Cycle of the Flea

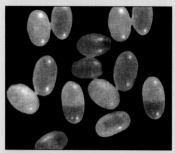

**Eggs**

**Larvae**

**Pupa**

**Adult**

Photos courtesy of Frelbusters*: Rx for Fleas.

# Flea Control

### IGR (INSECT GROWTH REGULATOR)

Two types of products should be used when treating fleas—a product to treat the pet and a product to treat the home. Adult fleas represent less than 1% of the flea population. The pre-adult fleas (eggs, larvae and pupae) represent more than 99% of the flea population and are found in the environment; it is in the case of pre-adult fleas that products containing an Insect Growth Regulator (IGR) should be used in the home.

IGRs are a new class of compounds used to prevent the development of insects. They do not kill the insect outright, but instead use the insect's biology against it to stop it from completing its growth. Products that contain methoprene are the world's first and leading IGRs. Used to control fleas and other insects, this type of IGR will stop flea larvae from developing and protect the house for up to seven months.

### *EN GARDE:*
### CATCHING FLEAS OFF GUARD!

Consider the following ways to arm yourself against fleas:
• Add a small amount of pennyroyal or eucalyptus oil to your dog's bath. These natural remedies repel fleas.
• Supplement your dog's food with fresh garlic (minced or grated) and a hearty amount of brewer's yeast, both of which ward off fleas.
• Use a flea comb on your dog daily. Submerge fleas in a cup of bleach to kill them quickly.
• Confine the dog to only a few rooms to limit the spread of fleas in the home.
• Vacuum daily...and get all of the crevices! Dispose of the bag every few days until the problem is under control.
• Wash your dog's bedding daily. Cover cushions where your dog sleeps with towels, and wash the towels often.

When treating with a household spray, it is a good idea to vacuum before applying the product. This stimulates as many pupae as possible to hatch into adult fleas. The vacuum cleaner should also be treated with a flea treatment to prevent the eggs and larvae that have been hoovered into the vacuum bag from hatching.

The second stage of treatment is to apply an adult insecticide to the dog. Traditionally, this would be in the form of a collar or a spray, but more recent innovations include digestible insecticides that poison the fleas when they ingest

PHOTO BY DWIGHT R KUHN

**Dwight R Kuhn's magnificent action photo, showing a flea jumping from a dog's back.**

the dog's blood. Alternatively, there are drops that, when placed on the back of the animal's neck, spread throughout the fur and skin to kill adult fleas.

### TICKS AND MITES

Though not as common as fleas, ticks and mites are found all over the tropical and temperate world. They don't bite, like fleas; they harpoon. They dig their sharp proboscis (nose) into the dog's skin and drink the blood. Their only food and drink is dog's blood. Dogs can get Lyme disease, Rocky Mountain spotted fever (normally found in the US only), paralysis and many other diseases from ticks and mites. They may live where fleas are found and they like to hide in cracks or seams in walls wherever dogs live. They are

**A brown dog tick, *Rhipicephalus sanguineus*, is an uncommon but annoying tick found on dogs.**

**The head of a dog tick, *Dermacentor variabilis*, enlarged and coloured for effect.**

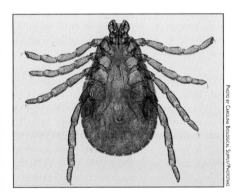

PHOTO BY CAROLINA BIOLOGICAL SUPPLY/PHOTOTAKE

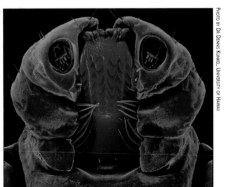

PHOTO BY DR DENNIS KUNKEL, UNIVERSITY OF HAWAII

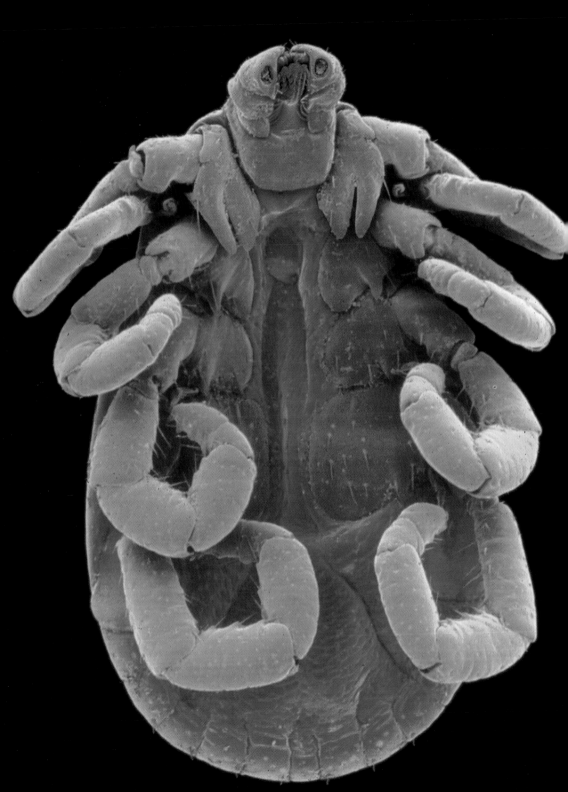

controlled the same way fleas are controlled.

The dog tick, *Dermacentor variabilis*, may well be the most common dog tick in many geographical areas, especially those areas where the climate is hot and humid.

Most dog ticks have life expectancies of a week to six months, depending upon climatic conditions. They can neither jump nor fly, but they can crawl slowly and can range up to 5 metres (16 feet) to reach a sleeping or unsuspecting dog.

## BEWARE THE DEER TICK

The great outdoors may be fun for your dog, but it also is a home to dangerous ticks. Deer ticks carry a bacterium known as *Borrelia burgdorferi* and are most active in the autumn and spring. When infections are caught early, penicillin and tetracycline are effective antibiotics, but if left untreated the bacteria may cause neurological, kidney and cardiac problems as well as long-term trouble with walking and painful joints.

Opposite page: The dog tick, *Dermacentor variabilis*, is probably the most common tick found on dogs. Look at the strength in its eight legs! No wonder it's hard to detach them.

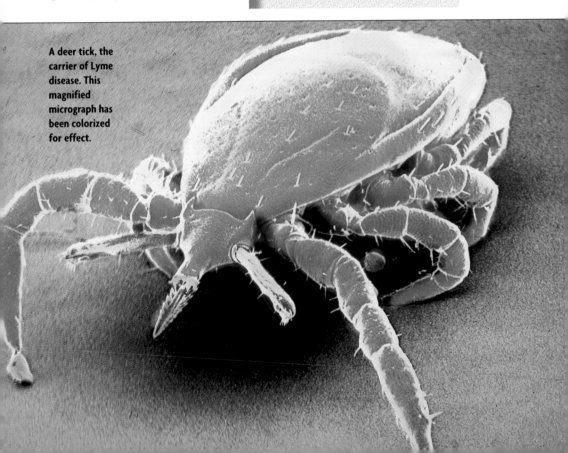

A deer tick, the carrier of Lyme disease. This magnified micrograph has been colorized for effect.

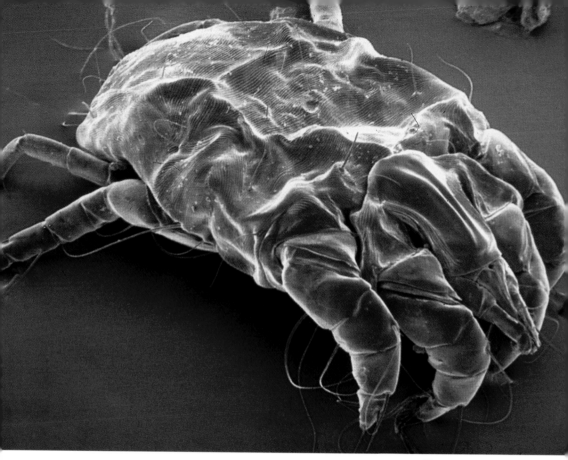

The mange mite, *Psoroptes bovis*.

Human lice look like dog lice; the two are closely related.

PHOTO BY DWIGHT R KUHN

### MANGE

Mites cause a skin irritation called mange. Some are contagious, like *Cheyletiella*, ear mites, scabies and chiggers. Mites that cause ear-mite infestations are usually controlled with Lindane, which can only be administered by a vet, followed by Tresaderm at home.

It is essential that your dog be treated for mange as quickly as possible because some forms of mange are transmissible to people.

## INTERNAL PARASITES

Most animals—fishes, birds and mammals, including dogs and humans—have worms and other parasites that live inside their bodies. According to Dr Herbert R Axelrod, the fish pathologist, there are two kinds of parasites: dumb and smart. The smart parasites live in peaceful cooperation with their hosts (symbiosis), while the dumb parasites kill their hosts. Most of the worm infections are relatively easy to control. If they are not controlled, they weaken the host dog to the point that other medical problems occur, but they are not dumb parasites.

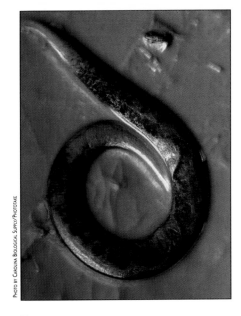

The roundworm, *Rhabditis*. The roundworm can infect both dogs and humans.

PHOTO BY CAROLINA BIOLOGICAL SUPPLY/PHOTOTAKE

### ROUNDWORM

Average size dogs can pass 1,360,000 roundworm eggs every day. For example, if there were only 1 million dogs in the world, the world would be saturated with 1,300 metric tonnes of dog faeces. These faeces would contain 15,000,000,000 roundworm eggs.

It's known that 7–31% of home gardens and children's play boxes in the US contain roundworm eggs.

Flushing dog's faeces down the toilet is not a safe practice because the usual sewage treatments do not destroy roundworm eggs.

Infected puppies start shedding roundworm eggs at 3 weeks of age. They can be infected by their mother's milk.

### ROUNDWORMS

The roundworms that infect dogs are scientifically known as *Toxocara canis*. They live in the dog's intestines. The worms shed eggs continually. It has been estimated that a dog produces about 150 grammes of faeces every day. Each gramme of faeces averages 10,000–12,000 eggs of roundworms. There are no known areas in which dogs roam that do not contain roundworm eggs. The greatest danger of roundworms is that they infect people too! It is wise to have your dog tested regularly for roundworms.

Pigs also have roundworm infections that can be passed to humans and dogs. The typical roundworm parasite is called *Ascaris lumbricoides*.

## DEWORMING

Ridding your puppy of worms is VERY IMPORTANT because certain worms that puppies carry, such as tapeworms and roundworms, can infect humans.

Breeders initiate a deworming programme at or about four weeks of age. The routine is repeated every two or three weeks until the puppy is three months old. The breeder from whom you obtained your puppy should provide you with the complete details of the deworming programme.

Your veterinary surgeon can prescribe and monitor the programme of deworming for you. The usual programme is treating the puppy every 15–20 days until the puppy is positively worm-free.

It is advised that you only treat your puppy with drugs that are recommended professionally.

## HOOKWORMS

The worm *Ancylostoma caninum* is commonly called the dog hookworm. It is also dangerous to humans and cats. It has teeth by which it attaches itself to the intestines of the dog. It changes the site of its attachment about six times a day and the dog loses blood from each detachment, possibly causing iron-deficiency anaemia. Hookworms are easily purged from the dog with many medications. Milbemycin oxime, which also serves as a heartworm preventative in Collies, can be used for this purpose.

In Britain the 'temperate climate' hookworm (*Uncinaria stenocephala*) is rarely found in pet or show dogs, but can occur in hunting packs, racing Greyhounds and sheepdogs because the worms can be prevalent wherever dogs are exercised regularly on grassland.

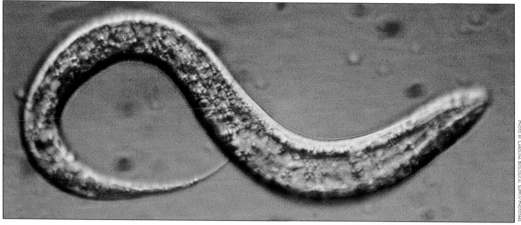

PHOTO BY CAROLINA BIOLOGICAL SUPPLY/PHOTOTAKE

The infective stage of the hookworm larva.

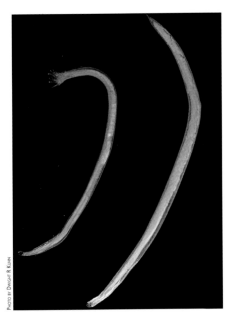

Photo by Dwight R Kuhn

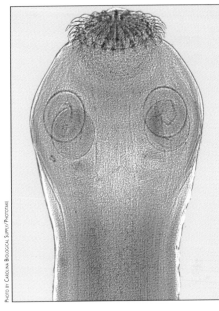

Photo by Carolina Biological Supply/Phototake

**Left:**
Male and female hookworms, *Ancylostoma caninum*, are uncommonly found in pet or show dogs in Britain. Hookworms may infect other dogs that have exposure to grasslands.

**Right:**
The head and rostellum (the round prominence on the scolex) of a tapeworm, which infects dogs and humans.

## TAPEWORM

Humans, rats, squirrels, foxes, coyotes, wolves, mixed breeds of dogs and purebred dogs are all susceptible to tapeworm infection. Except in humans, tapeworm is usually not a fatal infection.

Infected individuals can harbour a thousand parasitic worms.

Tapeworms have two sexes—male and female (many other worms have only one sex—male and female in the same worm).

If dogs eat infected rats or mice, they get the tapeworm disease.

One month after attaching to a dog's intestine, the worm starts shedding eggs. These eggs are infective immediately.

Infective eggs can live for a few months without a host animal.

## TAPEWORMS

There are many species of tapeworm. They are carried by fleas! The dog eats the flea and starts the tapeworm cycle. Humans can also be infected with tapeworms, so don't eat fleas! Fleas are so small that your dog could pass them onto your hands, your plate or your food and thus make it possible for you to ingest a flea that is carrying tapeworm eggs.

While tapeworm infection is not life-threatening in dogs (smart parasite!), it can be the cause of a very serious liver disease for humans. About 50 percent of the humans infected with *Echinococcus multilocularis*, a type of tapeworm that causes alveolar hydatis, perish.

## HEARTWORMS

Heartworms are thin, extended worms up to 30 cms (12 ins) long, which live in a dog's heart and the major blood vessels surrounding it. Dogs may have up to 200 worms. Symptoms may be loss of energy, loss of appetite, coughing, the development of a pot belly and anaemia.

Heartworms are transmitted by mosquitoes. The mosquito drinks the blood of an infected dog and takes in larvae with the blood. The larvae, called microfilaria, develop within the body of the mosquito and are passed on to the next dog bitten after the larvae mature. It takes two to three weeks for the larvae to develop to the infective stage within the body of the mosquito. Dogs should be treated at about six weeks of age, and maintained on a prophylactic dose given monthly.

Blood testing for heartworms is not necessarily indicative of how seriously your dog is infected. This is a dangerous disease. Although heartworm is a problem for dogs in America, Australia, Asia and Central Europe, dogs in the United Kingdom are not currently affected by heartworm.

The heart of a dog infected with canine heartworm, *Dirofilaria immitis.*

PHOTO BY JAMES E HAYDEN, RPB/PHOTOTAKE

# First Aid at a Glance

### Burns
Place the affected area under cool water; use ice if only a small area is burnt.

### Bee/Insect bites
Apply ice to relieve swelling; antihistamine dosed properly.

### Animal bites
Clean any bleeding area; apply pressure until bleeding subsides; go to the vet.

### Spider bites
Use cold compress and a pressurised pack to inhibit venom's spreading.

### Antifreeze poisoning
Induce vomiting with hydrogen peroxide. Seek *immediate* veterinary help!

### Fish hooks
Removal best handled by vet; hook must be cut in order to remove.

### Snake bites
Pack ice around bite; contact vet quickly; identify snake for proper antivenin.

### Car accident
Move dog from roadway with blanket; seek veterinary aid.

### Shock
Calm the dog, keep him warm; seek immediate veterinary help.

### Nosebleed
Apply cold compress to the nose; apply pressure to any visible abrasion.

### Bleeding
Apply pressure above the area; treat wound by applying a cotton pack.

### Heat stroke
Submerge dog in cold bath; cool down with fresh air and water; go to the vet.

### Frostbite/Hypothermia
Warm the dog with a warm bath, electric blankets or hot water bottles.

### Abrasions
Clean the wound and wash out thoroughly with fresh water; apply antiseptic.

 *Remember: an injured dog may attempt to bite a helping hand from fear and confusion. Always muzzle the dog before trying to offer assistance.*

# HOMEOPATHY:

## an alternative to conventional medicine

### 'Less is Most'

Using this principle, the strength of a homeopathic remedy is measured by the number of serial dilutions that were undertaken to create it. The greater the number of serial dilutions, the greater the strength of the homeopathic remedy. The potency of a remedy that has been made by making a dilution of 1 part in 100 parts (or 1/100) is 1c or 1cH. If this remedy is subjected to a series of further dilutions, each one being 1/100, a more dilute and stronger remedy is produced. If the remedy is diluted in this way six times, it is called 6c or 6cH. A dilution of 6c is 1 part in 1,000,000,000,000. In general, higher potencies in more frequent doses are better for acute symptoms and lower potencies in more infrequent doses are more useful for chronic, long-standing problems.

## CURING OUR DOGS NATURALLY

Holistic medicine means treating the whole animal as a unique, perfect living being. Generally, holistic treatments do not suppress the symptoms that the body naturally produces, as do most medications prescribed by conventional doctors and vets. Holistic methods seek to cure disease by regaining balance and harmony in the patient's environment. Some of these methods include use of nutritional therapy, herbs, flower essences, aromatherapy, acupuncture, massage, chiropractic and, of course the most popular holistic approach, homeopathy. Homeopathy is a theory or system of treating illness with small doses of substances which, if administered in larger quantities, would produce the symptoms that the patient already has. This approach is often described as 'like cures like.' Although modern veterinary medicine is geared toward the 'quick fix,' homeopathy relies on the belief that, given the time, the body is able to heal itself and return to its natural, healthy state.

Choosing a remedy to cure a problem in our dogs is the difficult part of homeopathy. Consult with your veterinary surgeon for a professional diagnosis of your dog's symptoms. Often these symptoms require immediate conventional care. If your vet is willing, and knowledgeable, you may attempt a homeopathic remedy. Be aware that cortisone prevents homeopathic remedies from working. There are hundreds of possibilities and combinations to cure many problems in dogs, from basic physical problems such as excessive moulting, fleas or other parasites, unattractive doggy odour, bad breath, upset tummy, dry, oily or dull coat, diarrhoea, ear problems or eye discharge (including tears and dry or mucousy matter), to behavioural abnormalities, such as fear of loud noises, habitual licking, poor appetite, excessive barking, obesity and various phobias. From alumina to zincum metallicum, the remedies span the planet and the imagination...from flowers and weeds to chemicals, insect droppings, diesel smoke and volcanic ash.

## Using 'Like to Treat Like'

Unlike conventional medicines that suppress symptoms, homeopathic remedies treat illnesses with small doses of substances that, if administered in larger quantities, would produce the symptoms that the patient already has. Whilst the same homeopathic remedy can be used to treat different symptoms in different dogs, here are some interesting remedies and their uses.

**Apis Mellifica**
(made from honey bee venom) can be used for allergies or to reduce swelling that occurs in acutely infected kidneys.

**Diesel Smoke**
can be used to help control travel sickness.

**Calcarea Fluorica**
(made from calcium fluoride, which helps harden bone structure) can be useful in treating hard lumps in tissues.

**Natrum Muriaticum**
(made from common salt, sodium chloride) is useful in treating thin, thirsty dogs.

**Nitricum Acidum**
(made from nitric acid) is used for symptoms you would expect to see from contact with acids such as lesions, especially where the skin joins the linings of body orifices or openings such as the lips and nostrils.

**Symphytum**
(made from the herb Knitbone, *Symphytum officianale*) is used to encourage bones to heal.

**Urtica Urens**
(made from the common stinging nettle) is used in treating painful, irritating rashes.

# HOMEOPATHIC REMEDIES FOR YOUR DOG

| Symptom/Ailment | Possible Remedy |
|---|---|
| **ALLERGIES** | Apis Mellifica 30c, Astacus Fluviatilis 6c, Pulsatilla 30c, Urtica Urens 6c |
| **ALOPAECIA** | Alumina 30c, Lycopodium 30c, Sepia 30c, Thallium 6c |
| **ANAL GLANDS** (BLOCKED) | Hepar Sulphuris Calcareum 30c, Sanicula 6c, Silicea 6c |
| **ARTHRITIS** | Rhus Toxicodendron 6c, Bryonia Alba 6c |
| **CATARACT** | Calcarea Carbonica 6c, Conium Maculatum 6c, Phosphorus 30c, Silicea 30c |
| **CONSTIPATION** | Alumina 6c, Carbo Vegetabilis 30c, Graphites 6c, Nitricum Acidum 30c, Silicea 6c |
| **COUGHING** | Aconitum Napellus 6c, Belladonna 30c, Hyoscyamus Niger 30c, Phosphorus 30c |
| **DIARRHOEA** | Arsenicum Album 30c, Aconitum Napellus 6c, Chamomilla 30c, Mercurius Corrosivus 30c |
| **DRY EYE** | Zincum Metallicum 30c |
| **EAR PROBLEMS** | Aconitum Napellus 30c, Belladonna 30c, Hepar Sulphuris 30c, Tellurium 30c, Psorinum 200c |
| **EYE PROBLEMS** | Borax 6c, Aconitum Napellus 30c, Graphites 6c, Staphysagria 6c, Thuja Occidentalis 30c |
| **GLAUCOMA** | Aconitum Napellus 30c, Apis Mellifica 6c, Phosphorus 30c |
| **HEAT STROKE** | Belladonna 30c, Gelsemium Sempervirens 30c, Sulphur 30c |
| **HICCOUGHS** | Cinchona Deficinalis 6c |
| **HIP DYSPLASIA** | Colocynthis 6c, Rhus Toxicodendron 6c, Bryonia Alba 6c |
| **INCONTINENCE** | Argentum Nitricum 6c, Causticum 30c, Conium Maculatum 30c, Pulsatilla 30c, Sepia 30c |
| **INSECT BITES** | Apis Mellifica 30c, Cantharis 30c, Hypericum Perforatum 6c, Urtica Urens 30c |
| **ITCHING** | Alumina 30c, Arsenicum Album 30c, Carbo Vegetabilis 30c, Hypericum Perforatum 6c, Mezerium 6c, Sulphur 30c |
| **KENNEL COUGH** | Drosera 6c, Ipecacuanha 30c |
| **MASTITIS** | Apis Mellifica 30c, Belladonna 30c, Urtica Urens 1m |
| **PATELLAR LUXATION** | Gelsemium Sempervirens 6c, Rhus Toxicodendron 6c |
| **PENIS PROBLEMS** | Aconitum Napellus 30c, Hepar Sulphuris Calcareum 30c, Pulsatilla 30c, Thuja Occidentalis 6c |
| **PUPPY TEETHING** | Calcarea Carbonica 6c, Chamomilla 6c, Phytolacca 6c |
| **TRAVEL SICKNESS** | Cocculus 6c, Petroleum 6c |

## Recognising a Sick Dog

Unlike colicky babies and cranky children, our canine kids cannot tell us when they are feeling ill. Therefore, there are a number of signs that owners can identify to know that their dogs are not feeling well.

**Take note for physical manifestations such as:**

- unusual, bad odour, including bad breath
- excessive moulting
- wax in the ears, chronic ear irritation
- oily, flaky, dull haircoat
- mucous, tearing or similar discharge in the eyes
- fleas or mites
- mucous in stool, diarrhoea
- sensitivity to petting or handling
- licking at paws, scratching face, etc.

**Keep an eye out for behavioural changes as well including:**

- lethargy, idleness
- lack of patience or general irritability
- lack of appetite, digestive problems
- phobias (fear of people, loud noises, etc.)
- strange behaviour, suspicion, fear
- coprophagia
- more frequent barking
- whimpering, crying

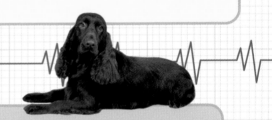

## Get Well Soon

You don't need a DVR or a BVMA to provide good TLC to your sick or recovering dog, but you do need to pay attention to some details that normally wouldn't bother him. The following tips will aid Fido's recovery and get him back on his paws again:

- Keep his space free of irritating smells, like heavy perfumes and air fresheners.
- Rest is the best medicine! Avoid harsh lighting that will prevent your dog from sleeping. Shade him from bright sunlight during the day and dim the lights in the evening.
- Keep the noise level down. Animals are more sensitive to sound when they are sick.

- Be attentive to any necessary temperature adjustments. A dog with a fever needs a cool room and cold liquids. A bitch that is whelping or recovering from surgery will be more comfortable in a warm room, consuming warm liquids and food.
- You wouldn't send a sick child back to school early, so don't rush your dog back into a full routine until he seems absolutely ready.

# CDS: COGNITIVE DYSFUNCTION SYNDROME
## 'OLD-DOG SYNDROME'

There are many ways for you to evaluate old-dog syndrome. Veterinary surgeons have defined CDS (cognitive dysfunction syndrome) as the gradual deterioration of cognitive abilities. These are indicated by changes in the dog's behaviour. When a dog changes its routine response, and maladies have been eliminated as the cause of these behavioural changes, then CDS is the usual diagnosis.

More than half the dogs over 8 years old suffer some form of CDS. The older the dog, the more chance it has of suffering from CDS. In humans, doctors often dismiss the CDS behavioural changes as part of 'winding down.'

There are four major signs of CDS: frequent toilet accidents inside the home, sleeps much more or much less than normal, acts confused, and fails to respond to social stimuli.

## SYMPTOMS OF CDS

### FREQUENT TOILET ACCIDENTS
- Urinates in the house.
- Defecates in the house.
- Doesn't signal that he wants to go out.

### SLEEP PATTERNS
- Moves much more slowly.
- Sleeps more than normal during the day.
- Sleeps less during the night.

### CONFUSION
- Goes outside and just stands there.
- Appears confused with a faraway look in his eyes.
- Hides more often.
- Doesn't recognise friends.
- Doesn't come when called.
- Walks around listlessly and without a destination goal.

### FAILS TO RESPOND TO SOCIAL STIMULI
- Comes to people less frequently, whether called or not.
- Doesn't tolerate petting for more than a short time.
- Doesn't come to the door when you return home from work.

The term *old* is a qualitative term. For dogs, as well as their masters, old is relative. Certainly we can all distinguish between a puppy Field Spaniel and an adult Field Spaniel—there are the obvious physical traits, such as size, appearance and facial expressions, and personality traits. Puppies and young dogs like to play with children. Children's natural exuberance is a good match for the seemingly endless energy of young dogs. They like to run, jump, chase and retrieve. When dogs grow older and cease their interaction with children, they are often thought of as being too old to play with the kids.

On the other hand, if a Field Spaniel is only exposed to people over 60 years of age, its life will normally be less active and it will not seem to be getting old as its activity level slows down.

If people live to be 100 years old, dogs live to be 20 years old. While this is a good rule of thumb, it is very inaccurate. When trying to compare dog years to human years, you cannot make a generalisation about all dogs.

Field Spaniels have a lifespan of approximately 14 years of age (range of 12 to 16 years), which is considerable for any pure-bred dog, regardless of size, lineage or utility. The typical age at which a dog is considered 'senior' status varies greatly. It is probably safe to say that by age 11 years, most Field Spaniels are retired or semi-retired from strenuous physical activities, though most appreciate being included in shorter and less strenuous sessions of a regular activity such as hunting. Keeping an ageing Field Spaniel active within reason is recommended for both mental and physical well-being.

Generally speaking, the first three years of a dog's life are like

**GETTING OLD**

The bottom line is simply that your dog is getting old when YOU think he is getting old because he slows down in his level of general activity, including walking, running, eating, jumping and retrieving. On the other hand, the frequency of certain activities increases, such as more sleeping, more barking and more repetition of habits like going to the door without being called when you put your coat on to leave the house.

seven times that of comparable humans. That means a 3-year-old dog is like a 21-year-old human. As the curve of comparison shows, there is no hard and fast rule for comparing dog and human ages. The comparison is made even more difficult, for not all humans age at the same rate...and human females live longer than human males.

## WHAT TO LOOK FOR IN SENIORS

Most veterinary surgeons and behaviourists use the seventh-year mark as the time to consider a dog a 'senior.' The term 'senior' does not imply that the dog is geriatric and has begun to fail in mind and body. Ageing is essentially a slowing process. Humans readily admit that they feel a difference in their activity level from age 20 to 30, and then from 30 to 40, etc. By treating the six- or seven-year-old dog as a senior, owners are able to implement certain therapeutic and preventative medical strategies with the help of their veterinary surgeons. A senior-care programme should include at least two veterinary visits per year, screening sessions to determine the dog's health status, as well as nutritional counselling. Veterinary surgeons determine the senior dog's health status through a blood smear for a complete blood count, serum

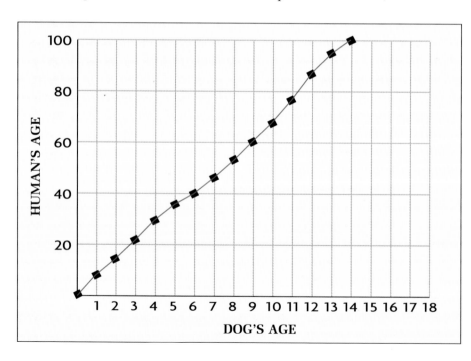

## SENIOR SIZES

While each dog ages at his own rate, the size of your dog does influence the age at which he will be considered a senior:

- dogs 20 lbs and under, 11–12 years
- dogs 21–50 lbs, around 10 years
- dogs 51–90 lbs, around 8 years
- dogs over 90 lbs, around 7 years

All figures are approximate and vary with each individual dog.

chemistry profile with electrolytes, urinalysis, blood pressure check, electrocardiogram, ocular tonometry (pressure on the eyeball) and dental prophylaxis.

Such an extensive programme for senior dogs is well advised before owners start to see the obvious physical signs of ageing, such as slower and inhibited movement, greying, increased sleep/nap periods and disinterest in play and other activity. This preventative programme promises a longer, healthier life for the ageing dog. Among the physical problems common in ageing dogs are the loss of sight and hearing, arthritis, kidney and liver failure, diabetes mellitus, heart disease and Cushing's disease (a hormonal disease).

In addition to the physical manifestations discussed, there are some behavioural changes and problems related to ageing dogs. Dogs suffering from hearing or vision loss, dental discomfort or arthritis can become aggressive. Likewise, the near-deaf and/or blind dog may be startled more easily and react in an unexpectedly aggressive manner. Seniors suffering from senility can become more impatient and irritable. Housesoiling accidents are associated with loss of mobility, kidney problems, loss of sphincter control as well as plaque accumulation, physiological brain changes and reactions to medications. Older dogs, just like young puppies, suffer from separation anxiety, which can lead to excessive barking, whining, housesoiling and destructive behaviour. Seniors may become fearful of everyday sounds, such as vacuum cleaners,

## SENIOR SIGNS

An old dog starts to show one or more of the following symptoms:

- The hair on the face and paws starts to turn grey. The colour breakdown usually starts around the eyes and mouth.

- Sleep patterns are deeper and longer, and the old dog is harder to awaken.

- Food intake diminishes.

- Responses to calls, whistles and other signals are ignored more and more.

- Eye contact does not evoke tail wagging (assuming it once did).

## NOTICING THE SYMPTOMS

The symptoms listed below are symptoms that gradually appear and become more noticeable. They are not life-threatening; however, the symptoms below are to be taken very seriously and warrant a discussion with your veterinary surgeon:

• Your dog cries and whimpers when he moves, and he stops running completely.

• Convulsions start or become more serious and frequent. The usual convulsion (spasm) is when the dog stiffens and starts to tremble, being unable or unwilling to move. The seizure usually lasts for 5 to 30 minutes.

• Your dog drinks more water and urinates more frequently. Wetting and bowel accidents take place indoors without warning.

• Vomiting becomes more and more frequent.

### AGEING ADDITIVES

A healthy diet is important for dogs of all ages, but older dogs may benefit from the addition of supplements like antioxidants, which fight the ageing process, and vitamin B, which aids the kidneys. Check with your vet before adding these or any supplements to your pet's diet.

body's vital organs. Some breeders recommend supplementing the diet with foods high in fibre and lower in calories. Adding fresh vegetables and marrow broth to the senior's diet makes a tasty, low-calorie, low-fat supplement. Vets also offer speciality diets for senior dogs that are worth exploring.

Your dog, as he nears his twilight years, needs your heaters, thunder and passing traffic. Some dogs have difficulty sleeping, due to discomfort, the need for frequent toilet visits and the like.

Owners should avoid spoiling the older dog with too many fatty treats. Obesity is a common problem in older dogs and subtracts years from their lives. Keep the senior dog as trim as possible since excessive weight puts additional stress on the

### HORMONAL PROBLEMS

Although greying is normal and expected in older dogs, a flaky coat or loss of hair is not. Such coat problems may point to a hormonal problem. Hypothyroidism, in which the thyroid gland fails to produce the normal amount of hormones, is one such problem. Your veterinary surgeon can treat hypothyroidism with an oral supplement. The condition is more common in certain breeds, so discuss its likelihood in your dog with your breeder and vet.

## COPING WITH LOSS

When your dog dies, you may be as upset as when a human companion passes away. You are losing your protector, your baby, your confidante and your best friend. Many people experience not only grief but also feelings of guilt and doubt as to whether they did all that they could for their pet. Allow yourself to grieve and mourn, and seek help from friends and support groups. You may also wish to consult books and websites that deal with this topic.

patience and good care more than ever. Never punish an older dog for an accident or abnormal behaviour. For all the years of love, protection and companion-ship that your dog has provided, he deserves special attention and courtesies. The older dog may need to relieve himself at 3 a.m. because he can no longer hold it for eight hours. Older dogs may not be able to remain crated for more than two or three hours. It may be time to give up a sofa or chair to your old friend. Although he may not seem as enthusiastic about your attention and petting, he does appreciate the considera-tions you offer as he gets older.

Your Field Spaniel does not understand why his world is slowing down. Owners must make the transition into the golden years as pleasant and rewarding as possible.

### WHAT TO DO WHEN THE TIME COMES

You are never fully prepared to make a rational decision about putting your dog to sleep. It is very obvious that you love your Field Spaniel or you would not be reading this book. Putting a loved dog to sleep is extremely difficult. It is a decision that must be made with your veterinary surgeon. You are usually forced to make the decision when one of the life-threatening symptoms listed above becomes serious enough for you to seek medical (veterinary) help.

If the prognosis of the malady indicates the end is near and your beloved pet will only suffer more and experience no enjoyment for the balance of its life, then euthanasia is the right choice.

#### WHAT IS EUTHANASIA?

Euthanasia derives from the Greek, meaning *good death*. In

## EUTHANASIA

Euthanasia must be performed by a licensed veterinary surgeon. There also may be societies for the prevention of cruelty to animals in your area. They often offer this service upon a vet's recommendation.

other words, it means the planned, painless killing of a dog suffering from a painful, incurable condition, or who is so aged that it cannot walk, see, eat or control its excretory functions.

Euthanasia is usually accomplished by injection with an overdose of an anaesthesia or barbiturate. Aside from the prick of the needle, the experience is usually painless.

### MAKING THE DECISION

The decision to euthanise your dog is never easy. The days during which the dog becomes ill and the end occurs can be unusually stressful for you. If this is your first experience with the death of a loved one, you may need the comfort dictated by your religious beliefs. If you are the head of the family and have children, you should have involved them in the decision of putting your Field Spaniel to sleep. Usually your dog can be maintained on drugs for a few days in order to give you ample time to make a decision. During this time, talking with

**TALK IT OUT**
The more openly your family discusses the whole stressful occurrence of the ageing and eventual loss of a beloved pet, the easier it will be for you when the time comes.

members of your family or even people who have lived through this same experience can ease the burden of your inevitable decision.

### THE FINAL RESTING PLACE

Dogs can have some of the same privileges as humans. The remains of your beloved dog can be buried in a pet cemetery, which is generally expensive. Dogs who have died at home can be buried in your garden in a place suitably marked with some stone or newly planted tree or bush. Alternatively, they can be cremated individually and the ashes returned to you. A less expensive option is mass cremation, although, of course, the ashes cannot then be returned. Vets can usually arrange the cremation on your behalf. The cost of these options should always be discussed frankly and openly with your veterinary surgeon. In Britain if your dog has died at the surgery, the vet legally cannot allow you to take your dog's body home.

Most pet cemeteries have suitable facilities for the storage of urns that contain the dogs' ashes.

Some sites in pet cemeteries are quite ornate.

### GETTING ANOTHER DOG?

The grief of losing your beloved dog will be as lasting as the grief of losing a human friend or relative. In most cases, if your dog died of old age (if there is such a thing), it had slowed down considerably. Do you want a new Field Spaniel puppy to replace it? Or are you better off finding a more mature Field Spaniel, say two to three years of age, which will usually be house-trained and will have an already developed personality. In this case, you can find out if you like each other after a few hours of being together.

The decision is, of course, your own. Do you want another Field Spaniel or perhaps a different breed so as to avoid comparison with your beloved friend? Most people usually buy the same breed because they know (and love) the characteristics of that breed. Then, too, they often know people who have the same breed and perhaps they are lucky enough that one of their friends expects a litter soon. What could be better?

### KEEPING SENIORS WARM

The coats of many older dogs become thinner as they age, which makes them more sensitive to cold temperatures and more susceptible to illness. During cold weather, limit time spent outdoors and be extremely cautious with any artificial sources of warmth such as heat lamps, as these can cause severe burns. Your old-timer may need a sweater to wear over his coat.

When you purchased your Field Spaniel you should have made it clear to the breeder whether you wanted one just as a loveable companion and pet, or if you hoped to be buying a Field Spaniel with show prospects. No reputable breeder will sell you a young puppy saying that it is *definitely* of show quality, for so much can go wrong during the early months of a puppy's development. If you plan to show, what you will hopefully have acquired is a puppy with 'show potential.'

To the novice, exhibiting a Field Spaniel in the show ring may look easy but it takes a lot of hard work and devotion to do top winning at a show such as the prestigious Crufts, not to mention a little luck too!

The first concept that the canine novice learns when watching a dog show is that each dog first competes against members of its own breed. Once the judge has selected the best member of each breed, provided that the show is judged on a Group system, that chosen dog will compete with other dogs in its group. Finally the best of each group will compete for

Best in Show and Reserve Best in Show.

The second concept that you must understand is that the dogs are not actually compared against one another. The judge compares each dog against the breed standard, which is a written description of the ideal specimen of the breed. While some early breed standards were indeed based on specific dogs that were famous or popular, many dedicated enthusiasts say that a perfect specimen, described in the standard, has never walked into a show ring, has never been bred and, to the woe of dog breeders around the globe, does not exist. Breeders attempt to get as close to this ideal as possible, with every litter, but theoretically the 'perfect' dog is so elusive that it is impossible. (And if the 'perfect' dog were born, breeders and judges would never agree that it was indeed 'perfect.')

If you are interested in exploring dog shows, your best bet is to join your local breed club. These clubs often host both Championship and Open Shows, and sometimes Match meetings and special events, all of which could be of interest, even if you are only an onlooker. Clubs also send out newsletters and some organise training days and seminars in order that people may learn more about their chosen breed. To locate the breed club closest to you, contact The Kennel Club, the ruling body for the British dog world.

The Kennel Club governs not only conformation shows but also working trials, obedience trials, agility trials and field trials. The Kennel Club furnishes the rules and regulations for all these events plus general dog registration and other basic requirements of dog ownership. Its annual show, called the Crufts Dog Show, held in Birmingham, is the largest benched show in England. Every year over 20,000 of the UK's best dogs qualify to participate in this marvellous show which lasts four days.

The Kennel Club governs many different kinds of shows in Great Britain, Australia, South Africa and beyond. At the most competitive and prestigious of these shows, the Championship Shows, a dog can earn Challenge Certificates (CCs), and thereby become a Show Champion or a Champion. A dog must earn three Challenge Certificates under three different judges to earn the prefix of 'Sh Ch' or 'Ch.' Of course the Field Spaniel, as a Gundog breed, must also qualify in a field trial in order to gain the title of full champion. Challenge Certificates are awarded to a very small percentage of the dogs competing, and dogs that are already Champions compete with others for these coveted CCs. The number of Challenge Certificates awarded in any one year is based upon the total number of dogs in each breed entered for competition.

There are three types of Championship Shows: an all-breed General Championship Show for all Kennel-Club-recognised breeds; a Group Championship Show, which is limited to breeds within one of the groups; and a Breed Show, which is usually confined to a single breed. The Kennel Club determines which breeds at which Championship Shows will have the opportunity to earn Challenge Certificates (or tickets). Serious exhibitors often will opt not to participate if the tickets are withheld at a particular show. This policy makes earning championships even more difficult to accomplish.

Open Shows are generally less competitive and are frequently used as 'practice shows' for young dogs. There are hundreds of Open Shows each year that can be delightful social events and are great first show experiences for the novice. Even if you're considering jus* watching a show to wet your paws, an Open Show is a great choice.

While Championship and Open Shows are most important for the beginner to understand, there are other types of shows in which the interested dog owner can participate. Training clubs sponsor Matches that can be entered on the day of the show for a nominal fee. In these introductory-level exhibitions, two dogs are pulled out of a hat and 'matched,' the winner of that match goes on to the next round, and eventually only one dog is left undefeated.

Exemption Shows are much more light-hearted affairs with usually only four pedigree classes and several 'fun' classes, all of which can be entered on that day. Exemption Shows are sometimes held in conjunction with small agricultural shows and the proceeds must be given to a charity. Limited Shows are also available in small number, but

entry is restricted to members of the club which hosts the show, although one can usually join the club when making an entry.

Before you actually step into the ring, you would be well advised to sit back and observe the judge's ring procedure. If it is your first time in the ring, do not be over-anxious and run to the front of the line. It is much better to stand back and study how the exhibitor in front of you is performing. The judge asks each handler to 'stand' the dog, hopefully showing the dog off to his best advantage. The judge will observe the dog from a distance and from different angles, approach the dog, check his teeth,

overall structure, alertness and muscle tone, as well as consider how well the dog 'conforms' to the standard. Most importantly, the judge will have the exhibitor move the dog around the ring in some pattern that he or she should specify (another advantage to not going first, but always listen since some judges change their directions, and the judge is always right!). Finally the judge will give the dog one last look before moving on to the next exhibitor.

If you are not in the top three at your first show, do not be discouraged. Be patient and consistent and you may eventually find yourself in the winning line-up.

Remember that the winners were once in your shoes and have devoted many hours and much money to earn the placement. If you find that your dog is losing every time and never getting a nod, it may be time to consider a different dog sport or just enjoy your Field Spaniel as a pet.

Virtually all countries with a recognised speciality breed club (sometimes called a 'parent' club) offer show conformation competition specifically for and among Field Spaniels. Under direction of the club, other special events for hunting, tracking, obedience, and agility may be offered as well, whether for titling or just for fun.

## WORKING TRIALS

Working trials can be entered by any well-trained dog of any breed, not just Gundogs or Working dogs. Many dogs that earn the Kennel Club Good Citizen Dog award choose to participate in a working trial. There are five stakes at both open and championship levels: Companion Dog (CD), Utility Dog (UD), Working Dog (WD), Tracking Dog (TD) and Patrol Dog (PD). As in conformation shows, dogs compete against a standard and if the dog reaches the qualifying mark, it obtains a certificate. Divided into groups, each exercise must be achieved 70 percent in order for the dog to qualify. If the dog achieves 80 percent in the open level, it receives a Certificate

**Since there are so few Field Spaniels entered in breed competition, it is considerably difficult to earn a championship.**

of Merit (COM); in the championship level, it receives a Qualifying Certificate. At the CD stake, dogs must participate in four groups: Control, Stay, Agility and Search (Retrieve and Nosework). At the next three levels, UD, WD and TD, there are only three groups: Control, Agility and Nosework.

Agility consists of three jumps: a vertical scale up a wall of planks; a clear jump over a basic hurdle with a removable top bar; and a long jump across angled planks.

To earn the UD, WD and TD, dogs must track approximately one-half mile for articles laid from one-half hour to three hours previously. Tracks consist of turns and legs, and fresh ground is used for each participant. The fifth stake, PD, involves teaching manwork, which is not recommended for any Gundog breed.

## AGILITY TRIALS

Agility trials began in the UK in 1977 and have since spread around the world, especially to the United States, where they are very popular. The handler directs his dog over an obstacle course that includes jumps (such as those used in the working trials), as well as tyres, the dog walk, weave poles, pipe tunnels, collapsed tunnels, etc. The Kennel Club requires that dogs not be trained for agility until they are 12 months old. This dog sport is great fun for dog and owner and interested owners should join a training club that has obstacles and experienced agility handlers who can introduce you and your dog to the 'ropes' (and tyres, tunnels, etc.).

Field Spaniels are very agile dogs and usually do well in agility trials.

## FÉDÉRATION CYNOLOGIQUE INTERNATIONALE

Established in 1911, the Fédération Cynologique Internationale (FCI) represents the 'world kennel club.' This international body brings uniformity to the breeding, judging and showing of pure-bred dogs. Although the FCI originally included only five European nations: France, Germany, Austria, the Netherlands and Belgium (which remains its headquarters), the organisation today embraces nations on six continents and recognises well over 300 breeds of pure-bred dog. There are three titles attainable through the FCI: the International Champion, which is the most prestigious; the International Beauty Champion, which is based on aptitude certificates in different countries; and the International Trial Champion, which is based on achievement in obedience trials in different countries. Dogs from every country can participate in these impressive canine spectacles, the largest of which is the World Dog Show, hosted in a different country each year. FCI sponsors both national and international shows. The hosting country determines the judging system and breed standards are always based on the breed's country of origin.

The FCI is divided into ten 'Groups.' At the World Dog Show, the following 'Classes' are offered for each breed: Puppy Class (6–9

months), Youth Class (9–18 months), Open Class (15 months or older) and Champion Class. A dog can be awarded a classification of Excellent, Very Good, Good, Sufficient and Not Sufficient. Puppies can be awarded classifications of Very Promising, Promising or Not Promising. Four placements are made in each class. After all sexes and classes are judged, a Best of Breed is selected. Other special groups and classes may also be shown. Each exhibitor showing a dog receives a written evaluation from the judge.

Besides the World Dog Show and other large all-breed FCI shows, you can exhibit your dog at speciality shows held by different breed clubs. Speciality shows may have their own regulations.

**The Field Spaniel's gait reveals the quality of its construction to the judge.**

# My Field Spaniel

PUT YOUR PUPPY'S FIRST PICTURE HERE

Dog's Name _____

Date _____ Photographer _____